BIBLE CRAFTS

BIBLE CRAFTS

Joyce Becker

Holiday House
New York

I dedicate this book to my family, my Kita K'tana classes, and to the ancestors who have been the source of my inspiration. Special recognition goes to my daughter, Leslie, for her sensitivity and expertise in helping to put this book together.

Library of Congress Cataloging in Publication Data

Becker, Joyce.
Bible crafts.

Includes index.
1. Bible crafts.   I. Title.
BS613.B4   745.5′0242   82-80820
ISBN 0-8234-0467-6   AACR2
ISBN 0-8234-0469-2 (pbk.)

FOREWORD

The crafts in this book are intended to stimulate memories of old Bible stories. People usually remember more from a "hands-on" approach than from just reading a book or listening to a story.

I hope this book will inspire people to go back to the Bible to learn more about past generations. There is gripping suspense in the lives of these ancient people. Their wonderful adventures rival any current mystery story.

The men and women in the Bible become "living" characters as they are re-created in clay, wood, fabric, and paper. They can be made as colorful as the stories about them. Creating an upturned mouth can make a character happy, a downturned mouth can show sadness or anger; placing two figures together can show love. Different costumes can show the country the figures are from, and the period of time in which they lived. People can create Bible heroes and heroines that can be seen, touched and held.

Because there are so many Bible stories from which to choose, I had to limit my selection. I chose only those characters and events from the books of Genesis through Jonah that I felt would appeal most to children. As a child turns to the first page of this book, he or she will hold hands with the past.

J.B.
Edison, N.J.
June 1981

CONTENTS

BIBLE CRAFTS

BEFORE YOU BEGIN

Since crafts projects can get messy, change into old clothes before you begin. Also, place newspapers on your work surface and lay out the materials you'll need for your project ahead of time. Many crafts items can be found at home; others can be bought locally at a variety, craft, or hardware store.

Read the directions through to the end so that you are familiar with each step. If a knife or other sharp object or stove are mentioned, ask an adult for permission to use them.

When you're finished, be sure that paint containers are cleaned and closed, brushes are washed, and all supplies are put back neatly. Roll up the papers that cover your work surface and throw them in the trash. Clean your hands and put away your work clothes.

Now you are ready to display your handiwork, and say with pride, "I made this."

The Creation and Adam & Eve

Everything has a beginning: the earth, people, language, and customs. People are always interested in how things were started. Here is a fascinating story, a Bible story, about the beginning of the world.

A long time ago, before there were people and animals, there was only darkness and water and, of course, God.

Then God said "Let there be light," and created the world's first day.

On the second day, God created the blue sky and white clouds, and He called them "Heaven."

On the third day, God created the land and seas and added fruit-bearing trees, green grass, and colorful flowers.

On the fourth day, God created the bright yellow sun, the silvery moon, and the sparkling stars.

On the fifth day, God created tiny fish, giant whales, and birds of all types and colors.

On the sixth day, God created each type of animal and the world's first man and woman.

Then, on the seventh day, God looked around and saw that His work was good. He blessed this day, made it holy, and rested from His work.

One of God's most beautiful creations was a garden called "Eden." The tree of life and the tree of knowledge of good and evil, the most fragrant flowers, and plump, juicy fruits grew there. A river with cool, clear water in which all kinds of fish swam flowed through the land. Among the birds and animals and trees lived the first man made by God. His name was Adam. Although Adam was surrounded by beauty, God saw that he was lonely. God made Adam a woman to love, and she was called Eve.

Adam and Eve were allowed to eat any fruit in the garden but that which grew on the tree of knowledge of good and evil. The serpent that lived in the garden tempted Eve to taste the forbidden fruit, and she in turn gave it to Adam. God saw this deed and was saddened. God punished the serpent from that time on by making it crawl on the ground and eat dust. God punished Adam and Eve by making them leave Eden and lose everlasting life.

What better way to begin creating with crafts than with the story of Creation?

Days of Creation Puzzle

Materials:

7 unlined index cards, 3″ x 5″ (7.5 cm. x 12.5 cm.)

pencil

ruler

felt-tip marking pens, different colors

scissors or craft knife

Optional: magazine pictures to illustrate each day of creation

Directions:

1. The seven cards are for the seven days of creation. Take the pencil and draw a crooked line down the center of each card. Make the lines different. On one side of each line, take the pencil and print what God created on that day. (You might want to use the ruler to make horizontal pencil lines so that your lettering will be even. You can erase the lines later.) On the opposite side, illustrate what was created on that day.
2. Using the marking pens, color in each drawing and trace around each word.
3. Cut each card apart along the curved line.
4. Reassemble by matching the picture to the words.

Scratch Art from Scratch

Materials:

1 piece of cardboard
heavy-duty aluminum foil, 2″ (5 cm.) higher and 2″ (5 cm.) wider than the cardboard
cellophane tape
newspapers

India ink
paintbrush
needle or an open paper clip

Directions:

1. Center the cardboard on the dull side of the foil. Fold the edges of the foil over the sides of the cardboard; tape down the foil.
2. Cover a work surface with newspapers. Place the cardboard on the newspapers, foil side up.
3. Using the brush, cover the surface with several coats of India ink. Let dry.
4. Take the needle or paper clip and gently scratch an appropriate design into the ink until the foil shows through. The fewer the lines, the more effective the design.

Drapery Ring Miniatures of Creation

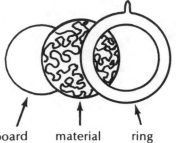

cardboard   material   ring

Materials:

7 drapery rings, stained, painted
  or unfinished
thin cardboard
pencil
scissors
material scraps

white glue
miniature objects (from craft
  store), magazine or handdrawn
  pictures
yarn, any color
decorative tacks (from variety or
  hardware store)

Directions:

1. Place the drapery rings on the cardboard. Trace around each of them with the pencil. Cut out each cardboard circle.
2. Place each cardboard circle on a piece of material, trace around the circle. Cut out each material circle.
3. To assemble the hanging, glue the material circle to the cardboard circle and then to the ring (figure A).
4. Arrange the objects and/or the pictures in the rings and glue to the material.
5. Thread a short length of yarn through the hole on top of the ring, and tie the ends.
6. Arrange the rings in a pleasing pattern. Hang each ring from a decorative tack.

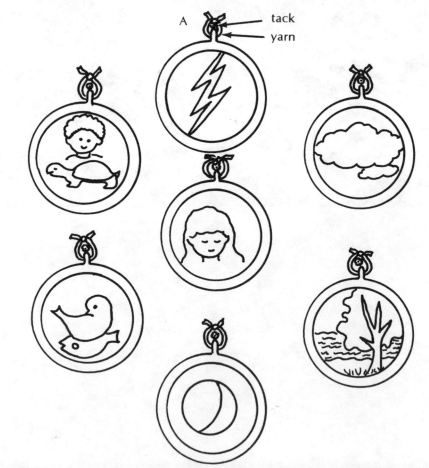

Dimensional Mirrored Plaque

Materials

1 framed mirror (with picture wire for hanging)

1 sheet of glass, cleaned, a little smaller than the mirror

paint that looks crackled when dry, or glass stain (craft store)

paintbrush

4 lima beans, beads, or tiny corks

white craft cement (craft store)

Directions:

1. Paint a picture showing each day of creation on one side of the sheet of glass. Let dry.
2. Glue a bean, bead or cork to each corner underneath the painted surface.
3. Attach the glass to the mirror by gluing the beans to the mirror's surface. Let dry before hanging. The mirror will reflect the picture, causing a double image.

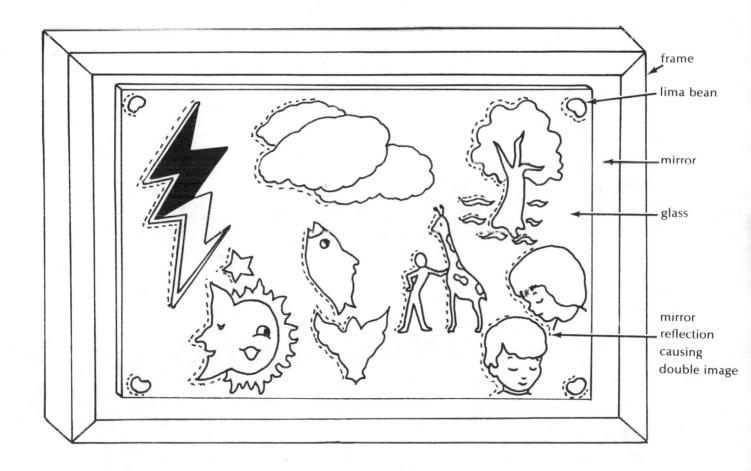

frame

lima bean

mirror

glass

mirror reflection causing double image

Day #1
He created the light.

A

Day #2
He created Heaven.

B

Day #3
He created plants, trees and seas.

C

Day #4
He gave the earth eternal light—the sun, stars and moon.

D

Day #5
He made the birds in the sky and the fish in the ocean.

E

Days of Creation Miniatures— Mobiles and a Stabile

Materials for first part of craft:

pencil
paper
plastic sheets that shrink (craft store)
permanent felt-tip marking pens, black and different colors

scissors
hole punch
cookie sheet covered with aluminum foil

Note: See materials below for second part of craft.

Directions:

1. With the pencil, draw a design for each day of creation on the paper. Figures A through G are suggestions. Make simple drawings since the completed picture will shrink to a fraction of its original size.
2. Place the plastic over the drawings. Using the black marking pen on the plastic, trace around the lines of the drawings beneath.
3. Turn the plastic over so the black outlines are face down. Using the colored marking pens, color in each drawing.
4. Cut out the drawings. Trim the excess plastic from each design.
5. Punch a hole near the top of each plastic piece.
6. Preheat the oven to 400° F. (205° C.)
7. Place the pieces, colored side down, about an inch apart on the foil-covered cookie sheet. Place the cookie sheet in the oven for a few minutes. The pieces will curl and then open as they shrink. Remove cookie sheet from oven and let the plastic cool before handling.

Materials for second part of craft:

fishing line (variety store, sporting goods store)
dowel (craft store, home supply store, lumberyard)
wire hanger
string
yarn, any color
screen (hardware store, home supply store)

plaster of Paris (hardware store, craft store)
wire (craft store, hardware store, variety store)
container for mixing plaster of Paris
stick for stirring
decorative container for stabile

Day #6
He created the animals and people.

F

Day #7
Shabbat—Day of Rest

G

Mobiles:

FISHING LINE AND WOODEN DOWEL MOBILE

Tie one end of the length of fishing line to a hanging ceiling fixture. Tie the other end to the center of a dowel. Add fishing line and dowels (figure H). Thread the loose ends of the fishing lines through the holes in the tops of the plastic pieces and knot. Adjust the fishing line until the mobile balances perfectly.

WIRE HANGER, STRING AND WOODEN DOWEL MOBILE

Bend a wire hanger into a circular shape representing God's world. Tie one end of string to the hook of the hanger; tie the other end to the center of a dowel. Add string and dowels (figure I). Keep the strings short so no part of the design will hang out of the "world." Thread the loose ends of the fishing lines through the holes in the tops of the plastic pieces and knot. Adjust the string until the mobile balances perfectly.

SCREEN AND YARN MOBILE

Tie a piece of yarn to each of the four corners of a large square of screen. Pull the ends of the yarn together above the screen and knot. Tie more yarn pieces to the corners and middle of the screen so that the loose ends hang down (figure J). Thread the loose ends of the yarn through the holes in the tops of the plastic pieces and knot. Adjust the yarn until the mobile balances perfectly.

Stabile

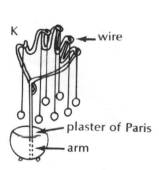

PLASTER OF PARIS AND WIRE STABILE

Shape a long piece of wire into a hand, leaving one end long. Twist the short end around the long one to make an "arm." Mix and pour the plaster according to package directions. Pour the plaster into the container and insert the "arm" before the plaster hardens. Curve the wire fingers and hang the designs from them (figure K).

Creation Wall Hanging

Materials:

pencil
paper
carbon paper
balsa wood, ¼″ (0.6 cm.) thick (craftstore, lumberyard, hardware store)
craft knife
fine sandpaper

acrylic paints, different colors
fine paintbrush
clear plastic spray (craft store)
shadow box frame (craft store, variety store)
white glue that dries clear
glue-on picture hanger (craft store)

Directions:

1. With the pencil, draw a design for each day of creation on the paper.
2. Using the carbon paper, transfer each design to the wood (figure A).
3. With the pencil, draw over the carbon lines of each design.
4. Using the craft knife, cut out each design.
5. Sand the edges of each wood cut-out.
6. Take the brush and decorate with acrylic paints. Let dry. Clean the brush with water.
7. Protect the cut-outs by spraying with a coat of the clear plastic. Let dry. Sand lightly, then apply a second coat and let dry.
8. Arrange the cut-outs within the frame and glue down (figure B).
9. To hang, attach the picture hanger to the back of the frame.

← paper with designs
← carbon paper
← wood

A

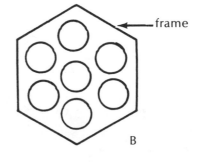

← frame

B

Woven Storyboard of the
Garden of Eden

Materials:

1 sheet of construction paper, 9" x 12" (23 cm. x 30.5 cm.), dark color

1 sheet of construction paper, 12" x 18" (30.5 cm. x 46 cm.), light color

ruler
pencil
scissors
cellophane tape
felt-tip marking pens, different colors

Directions:

To prepare the sheets for weaving:

1. Holding the 9" x 12" (23 cm. x 30.5 cm.) paper horizontally, use the pencil and ruler to draw a half-inch border all around (figure A).
2. Rule five vertical lines, spaced a half inch apart, inside each end of the border (figure B).
3. Cut along the vertical lines, as shown by the dotted lines in figure C.
4. Cut out five center boxes as shown by the dotted lines in figure D.
5. Cut five strips from the 12" x 18" (30.5 cm. x 46 cm.) paper, each measuring 1" x 18" (2.5 cm. x 46 cm.).

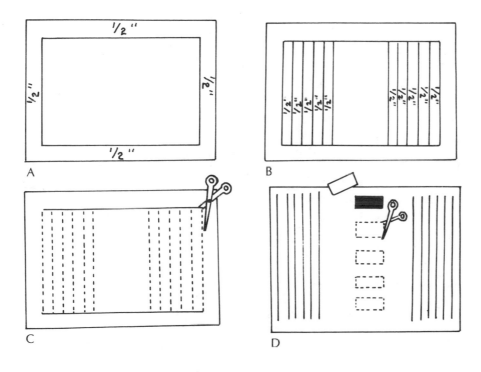

To make the weaving:

1. Weave the strips under one cut and over the next, and over the boxes (figure E).
2. Turn the weaving over, making sure the strips are still covering the open boxes. Place a strip of tape horizontally across the woven slats between each strip, as shown by the dotted lines in figure F.

To make the storyboard:

1. Adjust the ends of the strips that stick out so they are even.
2. On the top strip, make three drawings to illustrate the beginning of the Adam and Eve story. The drawings should be next to each other so that when the strip is moved from left to right, each drawing shows up in the box (figure G). Repeat the drawings in figures H, I, J, K on the other four strips. With the marking pens, color in the pictures.
3. Write the story that goes with each strip on either side of the box (figure L).

To operate the storyboard:

Start with the top strip. Pull each strip so the illustrations show through the "windows" as the story is told.

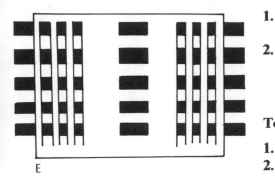

E

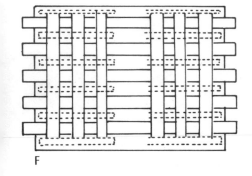

F

G

H

I

J

K

GARDEN OF EDEN

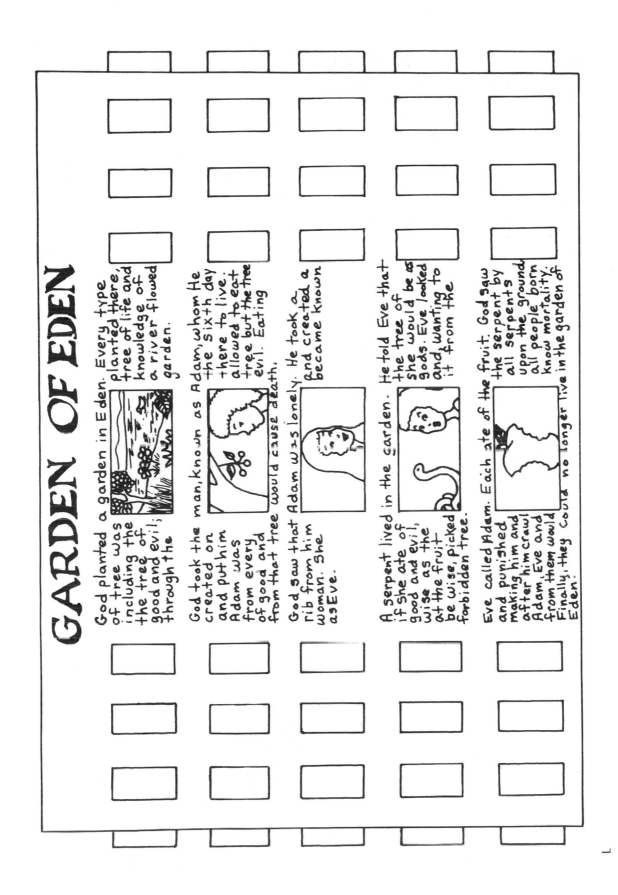

God planted a garden in Eden. Every type of tree was planted there, including the tree of life and knowledge of good and evil; a river flowed through the garden.

God took the man, known as Adam, whom He created on the sixth day and put him there to live. Adam was allowed to eat from every tree but the tree of good and evil. Eating from that tree would cause death.

God saw that Adam was lonely. He took a rib from him and created a woman. She became known as Eve.

A serpent lived in the garden. He told Eve that if she ate of the tree of good and evil, she would be as wise as the gods. Eve looked at the fruit, and wanting to be wise, picked it from the forbidden tree.

Eve called Adam. Each ate of the fruit. God saw and punished the serpent by making him and all serpents after him crawl upon the ground. Adam, Eve and all people born from them would know mortality. Finally, they could no longer live in the garden of Eden.

Stuffed Pictures of Adam and Eve

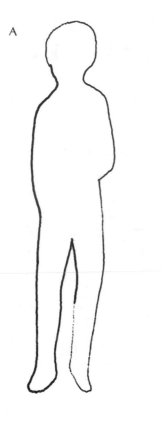

A

Materials:

frame with cardboard backing, any size (from variety or frame store)

patterned fabric to fit the frame

pieces of fabric in solid colors

scissors

spray adhesive (from craft or hardware store)

thread, same colors as fabric pieces

needle

cotton batting (from sewing or variety store)

white glue

glue-on picture hanger (craft store)

acrylic paint and brush, or felt-tip marking pens

jar of water

Directions:

1. Cut the patterned fabric to fit the cardboard backing of the frame.
2. Using the spray adhesive, glue the fabric to the cardboard.
3. Cut two identical figures of Adam (figure A) out of the solid-colored pieces of fabric. Place one cut-out on top of the other, right side out.
4. Using an overhand stitch (figure B), sew the cut-outs together. Stuff with cotton batting before sewing closed. Use enough batting to make the figures plump.
5. Repeat steps 3 and 4 to make Eve (figure C).

C

overhand stitch

B

6. With the white glue, glue the stuffed pictures to the fabric-covered cardboard.
7. Draw objects (tree, serpent, apple, flowers, sun) on the rest of the solid-color fabric pieces and cut out. Glue objects to the background. These don't need stuffing.
8. Add details to the pictures with acrylic paint or marking pens (figure D). (Clean brush in water before switching to different color of paint.)
9. To hang, attach the picture hanger to the back of the frame.

D

Vase with Clay Figures and Tissue-Paper Flowers

Materials:

1 box of multicolored facial tissues

spool of thin wire (craft store)

scissors

floral stems (craft store)

floral tape (craft store)

vase

clay that air hardens (craft store)

pointed stick

white glue

Optional: artificial leaves (craft store), perfume, acrylic paint, paintbrush

Directions:

1. To make one flower, take out ten tissues, open up the folds and separate the flattened tissues into two piles of five tissues each.
2. Gather each of the piles of tissues together in the center. Place one pile on top of the other to make an X. Bind the middles together with a piece of wire (figure A), keeping one end of the wire loose as a tail.
3. Twist the tail around a floral stem. Cover the wire and stem with floral tape (figure B).
4. If you want to add leaves, attach them to the stem with floral tape.
5. Carefully separate each layer of tissue to make a full, puffy flower.
6. Repeat steps 1 through 5 to make additional flowers. Place in the vase.
7. To add a garden scent, sprinkle or spray on a little perfume.
8. To make clay figures of Adam, Eve, the serpent, and the apple, use figures C, D, and E as patterns. Mold the clay into the shape of each pattern. Arrange the shapes on the vase and press gently. Use the pointed stick to add details. Remove the shapes from the vase. Let harden.
9. Paint the clay shapes if you wish. Let dry.
10. Glue the shapes to the vase. Let dry.

tissues

wire

A

Twist wire around stem.

floral tape

B

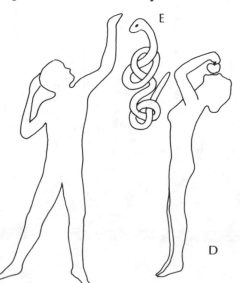

16

Stuffed Eve Stocking Puppet

Materials:

wire hanger
knee-high, light-colored stocking, adult size
cotton batting (from sewing or variety store)
rubber band

scissors or any sharp tool
large handkerchief
thread, any color
needle
felt-tip marking pens, different colors

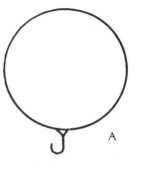

A

Directions:

1. Bend a wire hanger as shown in figure A.
2. Pull the stocking over the hanger and stuff with cotton batting (figure B); secure with rubber band at bottom as shown in figure C.
3. Using the scissors, poke a hole in the center of the handkerchief. Stick the hook of the hanger through the hole. Sew the handkerchief to the stocking (figure D).
4. With the marking pens, add features and hair to the stuffed head, and arms to the handkerchief body (figure E).
5. To make the head move, stick your hand under the handkerchief, and move the hook of the hanger back and forth (figure F).
6. To make an Adam puppet, repeat steps 1 through 4.

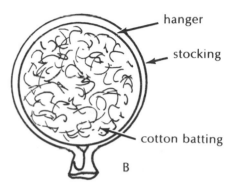

hanger

stocking

cotton batting

B

E

F

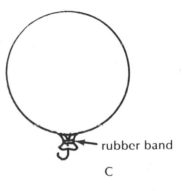

rubber band

C

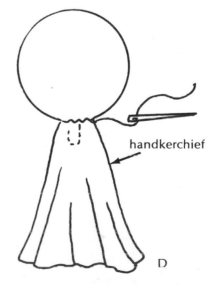

handkerchief

D

Sponge-Towel Flowers in a Garden of Eden Vase

A

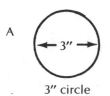

3" circle

B

Fold in half.

C

Fold in half again.

Materials:

1 roll of sponge towels, any color—looks similar to roll of paper towels (variety store)
scissors
floral wire (craft store)
floral tape (craft store)
artificial leaves (craft store)
1 piece of Styrofoam (craft store)

pretty container
thin cardboard
pencil
4 paper fasteners
felt-tip marking pens, different colors
white glue

Directions:

1. To make one flower, cut three circles, each 3″ (7.5 cm.) in diameter, from a sheet of sponge towels (figure A). Fold each circle in half (figure B) and then in half again (figure C).
2. Hold the three folded circles together and pinch the bottoms (figure D). Wrap with floral wire, leaving a loose end to serve as a stem (figure E).
3. Place the artificial leaves at the base of the flower. Wrap the stem of the leaves and the wire with floral tape (figure F).
4. Place the Styrofoam in the container. Insert the stem of the flower into the Styrofoam.
5. Continue making flowers until you have a full arrangement.

D

pinched bottoms

E

wire

F

leaves

floral tape

6. Using the pencil, copy the apple, serpent, and Adam and Eve patterns (figures G, H, I, J) onto the cardboard. Cut out each pattern.

7. Poke holes in the sides and arms of each body as shown in figures I and J.

8. To assemble, place the arms behind the body, lining up the holes. Put a paper fastener through the holes and close them loosely. If the arms do not move easily, enlarge the holes.

9. Arrange the shapes on the container (see figure K). Glue each shape, taking care to leave the arms free so they can move and reach for the forbidden apple.

10. Use the pens to add features, leaves for clothing, and other details.

G

H

I

J

Quilled Apple on a Garden of Eden Scene

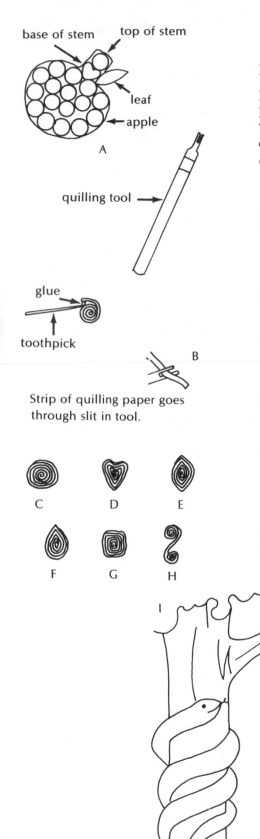

Actual pattern for apple

base of stem   top of stem

leaf

apple

A

quilling tool →

glue

toothpick

B

Strip of quilling paper goes through slit in tool.

C   D   E

F   G   H

Materials:

pencil
paper
waxed paper
cellophane tape
quilling paper, red and green (craft store)

quilling tool (craft store)
white glue
toothpick
predrawn picture of Garden of Eden or a picture of a garden cut from a magazine

Directions:

1. With the pencil, draw the outline of an apple on the paper, using figure A as a pattern. Tape waxed paper over the drawing. You should be able to see the design through it.
2. To make the apple as shown in figure A, cut sixteen 3″ (7.5 cm.) lengths from the red quilling paper. To make the base of the stem, cut one 3″ (7.5 cm.) length from the green quilling paper. To make the top of the stem, cut one 2″ (5 cm.) length from the green quilling paper. To make the leaf, cut one 6″ (15 cm.) length from the green quilling paper.
3. Slide one strip at a time into the slit of the quilling tool, and roll the paper around it (figure B). Slide the rolled strip off. To stop the strip from opening, tack down the open end with a dot of glue.
4. Leave all the apple shapes and the top of the stem shape round (figure C). Bend one round shape to make the stem (figure D). Bend one round shape to make the leaf (figure E). You may wish to experiment using one of the other basic quilling shapes (figures F, G, H). Let dry.
5. To fill in the pattern, glue the pieces together as shown in figure A.
6. Gently lift the dry, completed quilled apple off the waxed paper and glue it to your drawing (figure I).

Predrawn picture of tree, serpent, Adam and Eve. The apple is quilled and glued onto the drawing.

I

Noah's Ark

A long time passed after the creation of the Garden of Eden, and many people lived on earth. God looked upon their wicked ways, and He was sad. He spoke to Noah, whom He considered good, and instructed him to build an ark (a houseboat). God wanted to flood the earth so the evil people would drown. Noah's three sons, Ham, Shem, and Japheth, helped him make the ark large, strong and waterproof. When the ark was finished, God told Noah to take a male and female of every living creature onto the ark. Noah did as God asked and also brought his wife, his three sons, and their wives. When they were safely aboard, the rain began. The rain lasted for forty days and forty nights. Even the highest mountains were covered with water. Only those aboard the ark were saved. When the rain stopped, and the flood water dried up, the ark settled on the Mount of Ararat. Noah sent a raven out to check for dry land and then a dove. The dove flew out twice and returned the second time with a sign of land, an olive leaf. Noah released the animals, and he and his family said prayers of thanks to God for caring for them. In return, God told Noah and his sons to be fruitful and multiply and replenish the earth. Then He created a beautiful rainbow. This was His promise never to flood the earth again.

Try to feel what it must have been like to live in the days of Noah as you produce Noah, the ark and the animals in miniature.

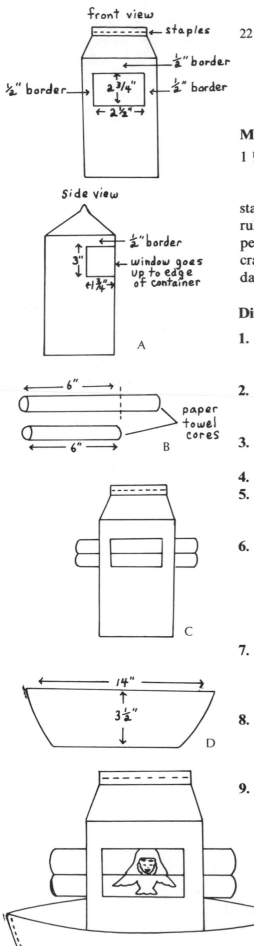

front view

← staples

½" border

½" border ← → ½" border

2¾"

2½"

side view

½" border

3"

window goes up to edge of container

1¾"

A

6"

6"

paper towel cores

B

C

14"

3½"

D

E

paper bag

staples

22

Funny Mixed-Up Noah's Ark

Materials:

1 ½-gallon (2-litre) empty, waxed milk or juice container, washed and dried
staple gun
ruler
pencil
craft knife or scissors
dark brown acrylic paint

wide brush
2 paper towel cores
white glue
2 sheets drawing paper
acrylic paints, different colors
fine brush
jar of water
1 large brown paper bag

Directions:

1. To make the top of the ark, close the container and staple to hold. Measure and cut out the windows from the front and sides of the container (figure A).
2. With the wide brush, apply a coat of dark brown acrylic paint to the container. Let dry. Clean brush with water. Repeat for a heavier coat.
3. Mark the paper towel cores to measure 6″ (15 cm.) in length and cut (figure B).
4. Glue drawing paper around each paper towel core.
5. Push the two paper towel cores, one on top of the other, through the side windows of the container. The cores will project from each side to serve as handles (figure C).
6. On the top core, using the pencil, draw the face of Noah or an animal; on the bottom core, draw the matching body. Turn the two cores until the drawings do not show. On the top core, draw another face; on the bottom core, draw the matching body. Continue until all sides of the cores are covered. You should be able to draw three different figures.
7. Remove the cores from the openings. Using acrylic paints and the fine brush, paint the drawings on the paper towel cores. Clean brush with water before switching to different color. Reinsert the cores into the container.
8. Cut a paper bag in half lengthwise. Place the two halves together. Measure and cut out the shape of the side of a ship (figure D). You should have two perfectly matched sides. Staple the sides together (figure E).
9. Mix and match the heads and bodies of the creatures by turning the cores.

Dimensional Noah's Ark Scene

Materials:

large box top
pencil
ruler
tracing paper
scissors or craft knife
white glue
rubber cement

cardboards in assorted thicknesses
white acrylic paint
paintbrush
glue-on picture hanger (craft or variety store)

Optional: black felt-tip marking pen

Directions:

1. With the pencil, draw a simple Noah's ark scene inside the box top.
2. Place tracing paper on top of the scene in the box and, with the pencil, trace around each figure and object in the drawing. Inside details, such as features and other markings, should be omitted. Remove the tracing paper and cut out each figure and object.
3. Use rubber cement to glue each of the tracing-paper cut-outs to a different thickness of cardboard. Cut around each drawing using the scissors or craft knife.
4. Place the cardboard cut-outs on the matching shape in the box top drawing and glue to hold. Let dry.
5. Paint the cut-outs and background white. Let dry. Clean brush with water.
   Optional: Add details, such as features, with the marking pens.
6. Attach the glue-on picture hanger and hang.

Colorful Feltboard Noah's Ark Scene

Materials:

1 large piece of heavy cardboad, any size

1 piece of light-blue felt, 4″ (10 cm.) larger in diameter than the cardboard

white glue

1 piece of thin cardboard, about the same size as the heavy cardboard

pencil

small pieces of felt (standard pre-cut sizes of different colors at craft store)

scissors

1 tube of liquid embroidery (craft store)

glue-on picture hanger (craft or variety store)

Optional: stiff brush

Directions:

1. Spread the light-blue felt on a table and center the heavy cardboard on it. Pull the felt over the edges of the board and glue down.
2. On the thin cardboard, draw pictures that tell the story of Noah and

the ark—Noah, his family, the ark, animals, clouds, raindrops, lightning, flood water, the sun, the raven, and the dove with an olive branch. Cut out each picture.

3. Select a small piece of felt for each cardboard shape. The felt should be an appropriate color for the shape—for example, orange felt for a sun, brown felt for an ark, and so on. Place the cardboard shapes on the felt pieces. Trace around the outlines and cut out.

4. With the tube of liquid embroidery, add details to the felt pictures.

5. Place the cut-outs in a pleasing arrangement on the light-blue felt-board and press gently in place. Peel the cut-outs off the felt-board. Arrange and rearrange them as different parts of the story of Noah are told. Show Noah and the animals around the ark with just the sun in a clear sky before the flood. Remove the animals, add water under the ark and raindrops and clouds in the sky to show the flood. Remove the rain and water and add the sun and rainbow to show the flood is over.

6. If the felt does not stick as well as it should, *gently* brush the back of the pieces to "rough up" the material.

7. Attach the glue-on picture hanger and hang.

Hanging Noah's Ark

Materials:

2 large round paper plates, about 9″ (23 cm.) in diameter
pencil
ruler
scissors

staple gun
felt-tip marking pens, different colors
hole punch
yarn

Directions:

1. To make the ark, take the pencil and draw a line across the center of one plate. Cut the plate in half. Keep one half for the bottom of the ark. Set the other half aside.

2. Take the other paper plate, and with the pencil, make a drawing (figure A).

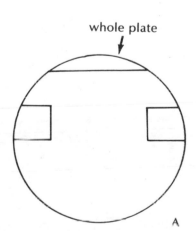

whole plate

A

3. Cut along the lines of figure A (figure B).
4. Draw windows with figures looking out of them (figure C).
5. Staple the bottom of figure C to the half plate you've saved for the bottom of the ark (figure D).
6. On the remaining half plate, draw animals as shown in figure E. Cut them out. Make slits by cutting along the parts of the animal that are shown by dotted lines (figure F).
   Optional: With the marking pens, color the animals and the ark.
7. Using the slits, place the animals so that they appear to be looking over the side of the ark. The monkey hangs by its tail (figure G). The animals may be stored by placing them in the pocket of the ark.
8. Punch a hole at the top of the ark. Thread a piece of yarn through the hole in the ark and knot it for hanging.

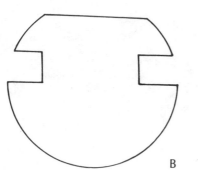

B

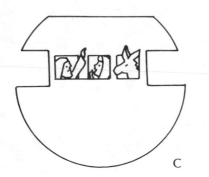

C

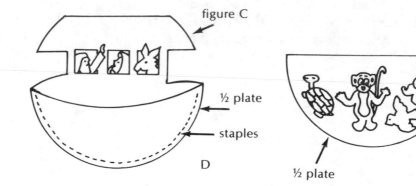

figure C

½ plate

staples

D

½ plate

E

F

G

Noah's Ark Diorama

Materials:

cigar box or similar box with flap
   lid
construction paper, white or beige
pencil
ruler
scissors

white glue
felt-tip marking pens, different
   colors, crayons or paints and
   brush
masking tape

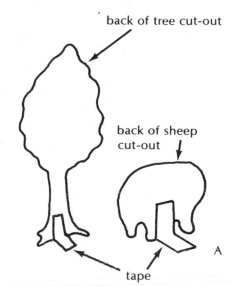

Directions:

1. Measure and cut drawing paper to fit the inside lid of the box. If there is writing on the inside or outside of the box, you may wish to cover that with paper, too. Glue to hold. Let dry.
2. With the pencil, draw a picture of the ark, the rainbow, and the dove with the olive leaf on the inside lid. With the marking pens, color the picture.
3. To make a gangplank, measure and cut out a strip of construction paper (see drawing of ark). Tape one end of the gangplank to the bottom of the door of the ark. Tape the other end to the bottom of the front of the box. The lid of the box will be held in an upright position by this strip of paper.
4. With the pencil, draw a picture of Noah, the animals, and scenery such as trees on a piece of construction paper. With the marking pens, color the pictures and cut them out.
5. Arrange the cut-out pictures in the box and tape each one in a standing position (figure A).
6. **Optional:** Print *Noah's Ark* directly onto the front of the box.

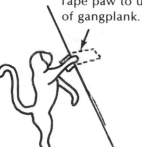

Tape paw to underside of gangplank.

NOAH'S ARK

Noah's Ark Mirrored Line Drawing

Materials:

framed mirror
drawing paper
pencil
carbon paper
masking tape

tube of liquid embroidery, any color (craft store)
craft knife, kitchen knife or razor blade
soft cloth
liquid window cleaner

Directions:

1. With the pencil, make a design of animals or use the one in figure A. Place the carbon paper, carbon side down, on the face of the mirror. Place the picture face-up on top of the carbon paper and tape the two to the mirror. (You will be able to trace the drawing without the paper sliding out of position.)
2. Pressing hard with the pencil, trace around the lines of the design. Remove the tape, drawing, and carbon paper.
3. Use the liquid embroidery according to directions on the tube to trace around the carbon lines on the mirror. To keep the carbon from smearing, place a clean sheet of paper over the lower part of the drawing. As you apply the liquid embroidery to the upper part of the drawing, rest the side of your hand on the sheet of paper. Move the paper down as you complete the drawing. Errors may be scratched off with a craft knife, kitchen knife or razor blade.
4. Fingerprints and carbon lines can be removed with a soft cloth and liquid window cleaner. Do not use an abrasive cleaner.

A

The Tower of Babel

As all things have beginnings, so too did language and nations. There was a time when everyone on earth spoke the same language. One day they decided to build a tower that could reach into Heaven. They used bricks and mortar and built the tower higher and higher. God became sad and angry when He saw how proud the people were becoming. It was not good for them to think they could reach Heaven.

To stop the building, God punished the people by making them speak different languages. Because they could not understand each other, they became confused. They could no longer work together, and the tower was never completed. The people left and spread out across the earth. Those who spoke the same language settled in the same parts of the world.

We remember how too much pride got these foolish people into trouble as we re-create the story in model form.

Eraser Print Tower

Materials:

1 oblong eraser
stamp pad
construction paper

acrylic paint, different colors
paintbrush
jar of water

Directions:

1. Press the eraser on the stamp pad. Then, press the eraser, inked side down, on the construction paper. Repeat until you have formed the shape of a tower.
2. With the acrylic paints, decorate the background with pictures of brick makers, bricklayers, overseers, the sun, and clouds. Clean the brush in water between applying colors.

Brick Sandpaper Tower

Materials:

coarse sandpaper   white glue
scissors   faces cut out of magazines
construction paper

  Optional: felt-tip marking pens, different colors

Directions:

1. Cut out many brick shapes from the sandpaper. The sandpaper will
    give the coarse texture of brick. Arrange the pieces, coarse side
    up, in the shape of a tower on the construction paper. Glue them
    down. Let dry.
2. Arrange the faces around the "brick" tower and glue them down.
    Let dry.
3. **Optional:** Using the marking pens, draw faces directly onto the con-
    struction paper.

Textured Picture of Tower of Babel

Materials:

1 large sheet of coarse sandpaper
crayons, different colors
1 sheet of construction paper, any color, larger than the sandpaper

glue
hole punch
yarn, any color

Directions:

1. On the rough side of the sandpaper, draw a picture showing people building the Tower of Babel. For an added effect, crayon the entire surface of the sandpaper.
2. Glue the completed drawing to the construction paper.
3. Punch a hole on opposite sides of the construction paper. To hang, thread the yarn through the holes and tie the ends together.

Stacked Boxes Tower of Babel

Materials:

boxes of different sizes
white glue
poster paint, any color that
   resembles brick
paintbrush

1   shallow container, several
    inches (centimeters) larger than
    the largest box
sand

   Optional: small artificial plants, such as for a fishtank (pet store),
   figures drawn on cardboard and cut out

Directions:

1. Turn the boxes upside down. Starting with the largest box and end-
    ing with the smallest one, stack them on top of one another. Glue
    them down. Let dry.
2. Paint the boxes. Clean the brush.
3. Spread the sand in the shallow container. Place the stacked boxes in
    the sand.
4. **Optional:** Add small artificial plants and cardboard figures.

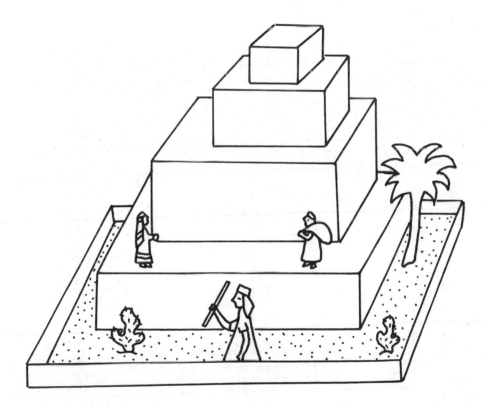

Tower of Babel in Clay Relief

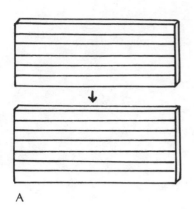

A

Materials:

Clay modeling compound that dries in the home oven (craft or hobby store). It comes in long, round strips that are attached.

kitchen or craft knife

wooden board, stained or covered with wood-grain adhesive-backed paper (variety store)

white glue

glue-on picture hanger (craft or variety store)

Optional: acrylic paint, any color that resembles brick, paintbrush

Directions:

1. Keep the clay strips intact as you remove them from the box. If you want the tower to be really high, use two sections of strips and attach them together (figure A).
2. Take the knife and, starting with the second strip from the bottom, cut away the clay so each strip becomes progressively smaller as you work up to the top (figure B).
3. To give the clay a brick appearance, make indentations with the knife.
4. Bake the clay according to package directions.
5. The clay may be left its natural color, or painted with acrylics.
6. Glue the clay tower to the board, and attach picture hanger.
7. **Optional:** Letters saying *Tower of Babel* may be shaped from clay, baked, painted, and glued to the board (figure C).

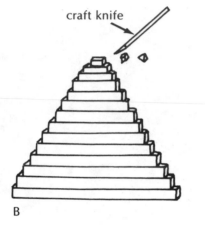

craft knife

B

C

Tin Can Tower that Rises

Materials:

construction paper, brick color
ruler
scissors
white glue

3 empty cans, 1 7 (207 ml.) oz. (tuna fish can), 1 10¾ (318 ml.) oz. (condensed soup can), 1 6 (177 ml.) oz. (tomato paste can)
hammer
nail
string

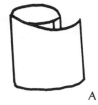

Optional: felt-tip marking pens, different colors

Directions:

1. Measure and cut a piece of construction paper to fit around one can. The ends should overlap (figure A). Glue to hold. Repeat with the other two cans. Let dry.
2. Using the hammer and nail, hammer a hole into the opposite sides of each can. They should be one-quarter inch (0.6 cm.) from the top. You'll have to hammer through the construction paper (figure B).
3. Hammer a hole one-quarter inch (0.6 cm.) up from the opposite sides of the bottom of the 10¾ (318 ml.) oz. can and the 6 oz. can (figure C).

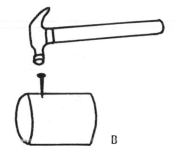

To assemble the tower:

1. Line up the holes of the 7 (207 ml.) oz. can with the bottom holes of the 10¾ (318 ml.) oz. can and attach with string (figure D). Knot the ends of the string to hold in place.

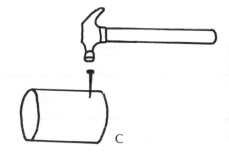

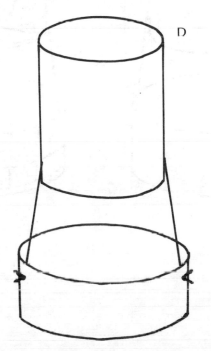

2. Line the top holes of the 10¾ (318 ml.) oz. can with the bottom holes of the 6 (177 ml.) oz. can and attach with string (figure E). Add a string handle as shown in figure F.

3. To make the tower rise, pull up on the string handle. Collapse the tower by lowering the string (figure F).

   Optional: Using the marking pens, add details to the construction paper such as bricks and people working.

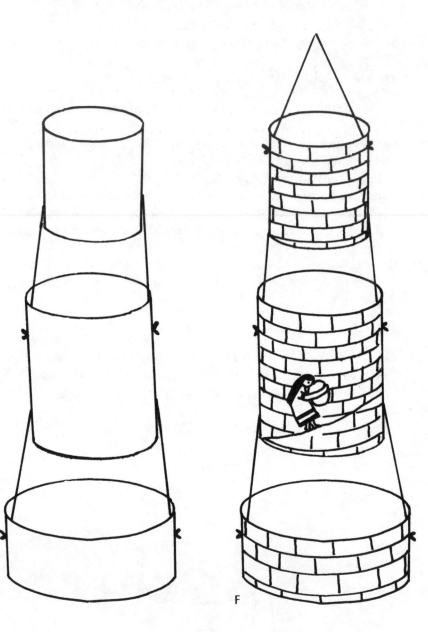

E   F

Tower of Babel Storyboard

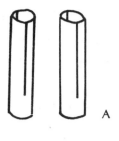

A

Materials:

4 empty toilet tissue rolls
scissors
acrylic paint, any color
paintbrush

3 sheets of lightweight cardboard
4" x 10", 4" x 8", 4" x 6" (10
cm. x 25 cm.; 10 cm. x 20 cm.;
10 cm. x 15 cm.)
felt-tip marking pens, different
colors

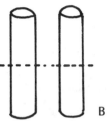

B

Directions:

1. With the scissors, cut slits into opposite sides of two toilet tissue rolls (figure A). They should extend down about three-quarters of the roll.
2. Cut the remaining two toilet tissue rolls in half to make four (figure B). Cut slits into the opposite ends of those, taking care that the cuts do not meet (figure C).
3. Paint each cardboard roll. Let dry.
4. Write the Tower of Babel story on the three sheets of cardboard. Start with the smallest sheet and finish with the largest one.
5. Insert the cardboard storyboards into the slits of the cardboard rolls (figure D).

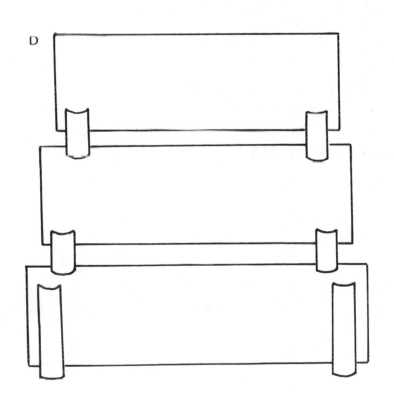

Foreign Newspaper Tower

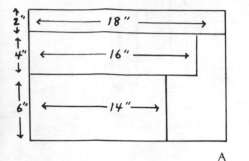

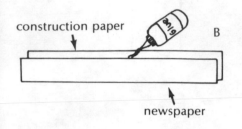

A

Materials:

construction paper, 12″ x 18″ (30.5 cm. x 46 cm.)
pencil
ruler
scissors

newspapers in different languages (i.e., English, Hebrew, Italian, Chinese—from different newsstands)
white glue

Optional: felt-tip marking pens, crayons or acrylic paint and paintbrush

Directions:

1. Measure and cut three strips from the 12″ x 18″ (30.5 cm. x 46 cm.) paper. The first strip should measure 2″ x 18″ (5 cm. x 46 cm.). The second strip should measure 4″ x 16″ (10 cm. x 40.6 cm.). The third strip should measure 6″ x 14″ (15 cm. x 35.5 cm.) (figure A).

2. Place the 2″ x 18″ (5 cm. x 46 cm.) strip on one of the newspapers, trace around it and cut it out. Glue the cut-out newspaper to the construction paper strip (figure B).

3. Repeat step 2 for the second and third strip using a different language newspaper for each.

4. Shape each strip, newspaper side out, into a circle and glue the ends together.

5. To assemble the tower, place the circles inside each other (figure C). If you want to make the tower higher, make additional circles.

6. **Optional:** Add people and draw in bricks with marking pens, crayons, or paint.

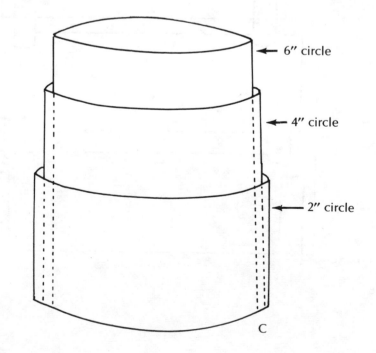

Abraham, Sarah and Isaac

A long time after Noah and the ark there lived a man by the name of Abram who often prayed to God. God saw that Abram was good and blessed him. He gave him the land of Hebron, where Abram built God an altar. In this land, Abram and his wife, Sarai, grew lonely and prayed for a child. God told Abram to have faith and that from then on Abram would be called Abraham, and Sarai, Sarah.

Even though Abraham and Sarah were old, God promised they'd have a son who was to be called Isaac. Three angels came to confirm God's good news. Sarah had the child and named him Isaac which means "he will laugh." Abraham loved him a great deal. But one day God tested Abraham's faith by asking him to offer Isaac as a sacrifice. Abraham's faith was so great that he was willing to do so. While he was getting ready, an angel came to Abraham and told him to sacrifice a ram instead, since God was pleased with his loyalty. Then the Lord blessed Abraham and all his people.

After we read about Abraham and Sarah and become inspired by their heroism, it is a good time to start creating.

Mounted Picture of Abraham in Relief (*Repoussé*)

Repoussé is the French word for a picture that is shaped or formed in relief.

Materials:

1 print of Abraham (religious calendars are a good source)
scissors
pan of water
paper towel
instant papier maché (craft store)
plastic bag

flat toothpick
stained plaque of wood (craft store)
clear plastic spray
glue-on picture hanger (craft or variety store)

Directions:

1. Cut out the portion of the print you want to use and discard the rest.
2. Place the cut-out picture in the pan of water for 15 to 30 minutes depending on the thickness of the paper. Remove the picture from the water. Place it on the paper towel to absorb excess water.
3. Put about 1 cup of papier maché into the plastic bag. Add water and knead, until it develops a claylike consistency. (Check package directions.) Mix more if needed.
4. Place the print face down on your work surface. Cover the back of it with ¼″ (0.6 cm.) layer of maché, spreading it to the edge of the print.

5. Turn the print over and place it on the wooden plaque. To model the print, round the edges of it with your fingers. With your fingertips, or the wide end of the toothpick, gently press areas you want indented. Use the toothpick to remove excess maché that has oozed out from the edges of the print. Let dry.
6. Apply several light coats of clear plastic spray. Let dry.
7. To hang, attach the picture hanger.

Styrofoam Abraham and the Three Angels

Materials:

Styrofoam meat trays
pencil
scissors

pan of hot water
white glue
large Styrofoam tray

Directions:

1. Draw the basic shape of a figure on a Styrofoam meat tray (figure A).
2. Cut out the pencilled shape.
3. Repeat steps 1 and 2 to make three additional figures.
4. Dip one cut-out figure into the hot water for a minute or two. Remove it from the water and immediately fold the head slightly down, the legs back at the knees and the hands forward into a praying position (figure B). Redip the figure several times to soften the Styrofoam if necessary.
5. Glue the figures in place on the large Styrofoam tray. A drop of glue between the hands will also make them stick together in a praying position.

B

The Three Angels

Materials:

Styrofoam ball, about 1½″ (3.8 cm.) in diameter (craft store)

cotton

fabric, white

white thread

wire, 2 4½″ (11.4 cm.) lengths, sturdy but pliable

cardboard

pencil

scissors

staple gun

white glue

black felt-tip marking pen

white felt

Optional: acrylic paint (flesh color), brush, needle

Directions:

1. To make the head, cover the Styrofoam ball with cotton. Cover this padded ball with fabric, gather it at the neck, and tie with thread (figure A).

2. To make the arms, insert the two 4½″ (11.4 cm.) lengths of wire into the fabric which is gathered at the bottom of the head. Stretch the wires out at shoulder height.
3. With the pencil, copy figure B onto cardboard and cut out.
4. Copy figure C onto cardboard and cut out. Place the cardboard pattern on the fabric, trace around the edges and cut out the robe. Repeat to make a second fabric cut-out of figure C.
5. Poke two holes through the cardboard body (figure B) about one-half inch (1.3 cm.) down from the top and centered about one inch (2.5 cm.) apart. Put a wire arm through each hole. Roll the "body" into a cone shape and staple closed.

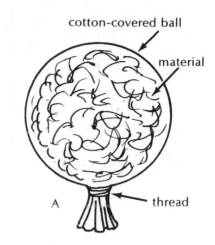

cotton-covered ball

material

A thread

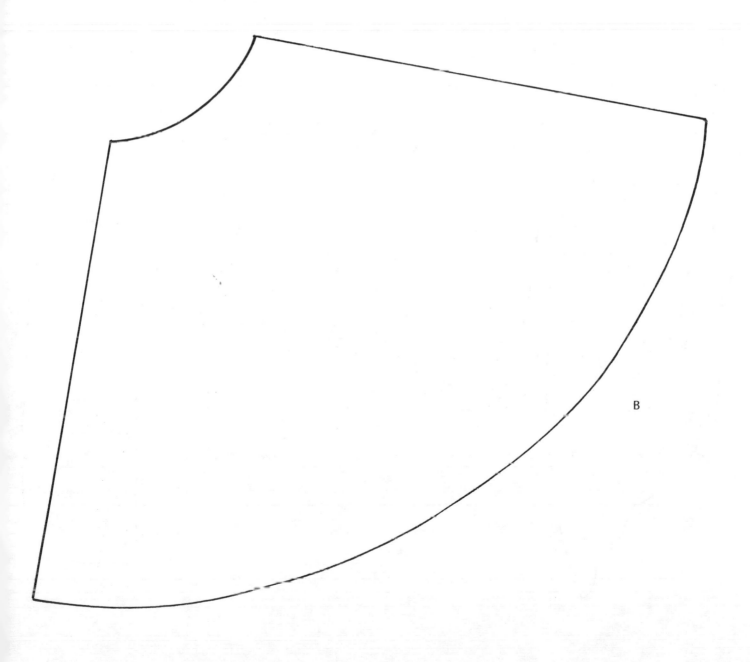

B

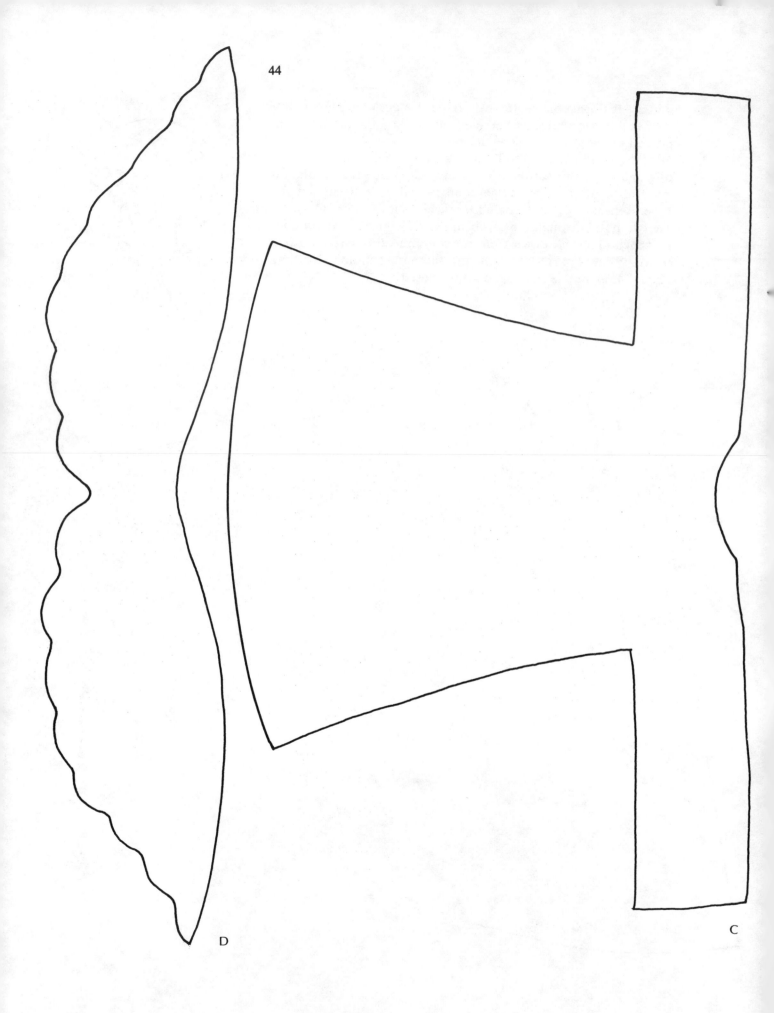

44

D

C

6. Place one fabric cut-out on each side of the cone-and-wire body. Glue or sew their sides together. The arms may be bent in any position.
7. Glue on cotton hair and beard.
8. Draw a face with the black marking pen.
9. To make the wings, trace figure D onto cardboard and cut out. Place the cardboard pattern on the felt, trace around the edges and cut out the wings. Glue them to the back of the angel.
10. **Optional:** Use figure E to make cardboard hands and feet. Cut out four hands and two feet. Glue one hand cut-out to each side of each wire hand. Glue the edges of the cardboard hand cut-outs together. Glue the feet to the underside of the base of the cone body. Bend the feet up so they show from under the skirt.
11. Repeat the necessary steps to make two more angels.

foot ⟶

hand ⟶

E

Wooden Plaque of Sarah and Isaac

A

Materials:

balsa wood, ½" x 3" x 6" (1.3 cm. x 7.6 cm. x 15 cm.) (craft store)
pencil
long screw
hammer
nail

crayons (different colors), sheet of paper and iron or wood stain (craft store) and a rag
glue-on picture hanger (craft or variety store)

Directions:

1. With a pencil, draw a simple, undetailed picture on the wood of Sarah and Isaac.
2. To make the design raised, turn the screw upside down, so that the head is against the wood and the pointed end is sticking up. Hammer the head into the wood to make an indentation. Go all around the pencilled outline (figure A). When done, the entire background will be indented.

3. Add details to the figures by scratching lines in the wood with the pointed end of the nail (figure B).
4. There are two methods of coloring the plaque.
    a. You can use crayons, but only on the raised figures. They will not work well on the background. Be sure to press down firmly. To set the color and make it look like paint, cover the wood block with the sheet of paper. Set the iron to the "wool" setting and turn it on. Place the heated iron on the paper-covered wood and hold it there until you see the wax being absorbed by the paper. Change the paper, and iron again. Continue until no wax comes off on the paper. To be extra safe, have an adult supervise the ironing process.
    b. Another way to color the plaque is to dip the end of a rag into stain. Lightly rub the stain over the wood, coating all the raised portions as well as the indented background. To make the completed plaque look more finished, stain the edges of the wood.
5. To hang, attach the picture hanger.

B

Walnut-Head Doll of Sarah

Materials:

1 walnut
nutcracker
2 chenille craft stems, 12″ (30.5 cm.) long (craft store)
white glue

cotton ball
scrap fabric or a small child's handkerchief
felt-tip marking pens (fine point)

> **Optional:** needle and thread, doll's bench (handmade or store-bought)

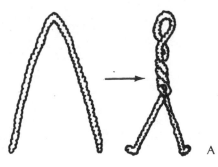

A

Directions:

1. Split the walnut in half. Remove the meat.
2. To make the body, fold one chenille stem in half. Leaving a loop on top, twist the stems together going about one-half way down. Separate the untwisted stems to form legs. Bend the bottom of the legs up to form the feet (figure A).
3. To make the arms, fold the remaining chenille stem in half and twist both sides together. Push the twisted stem through the loop in the body so that an even amount sticks out from each side. Cross one arm over the other and press to hold. Bend the end of each arm up to form hands (figure B).
4. To put the doll together, glue the loop of the body inside a shell. Glue the two half shells together. Let dry. The markings on the walnut give an aged look to Sarah's face (figure C).
5. Glue on cotton hair.
6. To dress the doll, wrap it in fabric, gluing or sewing to hold.
7. Draw a face on the doll.
8. **Optional:** Seat the doll on a doll's bench.

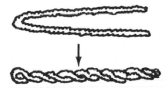

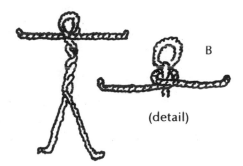

B

(detail)

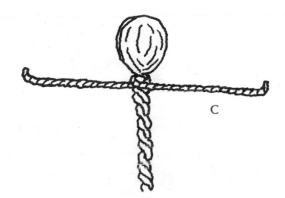

C

Fabric-Dressed Figure of Abraham or Sarah

Materials:

1 print of Abraham or Sarah (old calendars are a good source)
scraps of fabric
scissors
white glue

a frame that will fit around the print, a piece of stained wood or a piece of painted heavy cardboard on which to mount the print, or a box top in which to mount the print
glue-on picture hanger (craft or variety store)

Optional: lace, ribbon, silky trim

Directions:

1. Cut out the portion of the print you want to use and discard the rest. You might want to cut out two separate pictures of Abraham and Sarah, and then tape them together to form one picture.

2. To "dress" the figure in the picture, cut one or several pieces of fabric large enough to cover the clothing of the figure. Glue the cutout material to the figure. **Optional:** Add lace, ribbon or silky trim (for beard and hair).

3. Place the print in the frame, center it on the wood or cardboard, or mount it inside the boxtop, and glue to hold.

4. Attach the glue-on picture hanger and hang.

Jacob's Ladder

Rebecca, Isaac's wife, gave birth to twin boys. The first baby was covered with red hair, and he was named Esau. The second baby was born holding Esau's heel, and he was called Jacob. Isaac favored Esau, who grew up to be a hunter, while Rebecca was fondest of Jacob, who grew up to be a shepherd.

One day when Esau was hunting, he grew faint with hunger. He went to Jacob and begged for food. Jacob agreed to feed him only if Esau would give up the rights that belonged to him as the first-born son. Jacob had always been jealous of those rights. Esau was so hungry that he agreed to Jacob's request.

When Isaac was old and blind, he asked Esau to go hunting and bring him back some meat to eat so he could bless him before he died. Since Rebecca favored Jacob, she didn't want Esau to be blessed and thought of a way of tricking Isaac into thinking Jacob was Esau.

She covered Jacob's hands and neck with goat's skin and gave him some delicious meat to bring to his father. Jacob went to his father who touched him, thinking he was Esau because the goat skin made him hairy. When Esau returned with meat for his father and discovered the trick that Jacob had played, he was furious!

To escape Esau's anger, Jacob left to live with his uncle. One night, during the journey, he lay down and rested his head on a stone. He fell asleep and dreamt a strange dream. God's angels were climbing up and down a ladder that reached to Heaven. Jacob heard God's voice bless him and his children after him.

In the morning, Jacob remembered the dream and God's blessing. He made a promise, saying that if God would guard him on his trip and give him food and clothes and bring him safely home to his father's house, then God would be his Lord.

Now that we have read about Jacob and his family, let the crafts in this chapter become a link that connects us to the past.

Dimensional Jacob's Ladder
Shoe Box Scene (1)

A

B

Materials:

shoe box, any size
acrylic or poster paint, blue and
  green
paintbrush
heavy paper or poster board
pencil
crayons, different colors

scissors
ruler
white glue
string
small stone
green construction paper

Directions:

1. Place the shoe box without its top on its side. Paint or color the inside top, back and sides of the box blue and the bottom green.
2. Using heavy paper or poster board, draw, color and cut out clouds, a ladder (measured to fit the inside height of the box), tiny angels and Jacob (figures A, B, C, D).
3. Glue one end of a short length of string to a cloud and the other end to the inside top of the box.
4. Glue the top of the ladder to the top of the box, and the bottom to the bottom of the box.
5. Glue the angels to the ladder.
6. Glue the cut-out of Jacob to the bottom of the box.
7. Glue the stone to Jacob's head and to the bottom of the box.
8. Measure and cut out a narrow strip of the green construction paper to fit the inside width of the box. Fringe one end of the strip to look like grass (figure E), and glue it across the bottom front of the box.

C

D

"grass"
E

Dimensional Jacob's Ladder
Shoe Box Scene (2)

Materials:

shoe box top
aluminum foil
potting soil (garden supply store)
grass seed (garden supply store)
large jar top
nonhardening clay, plasteline, (hobby store)

thin sticks (hobby store), paper straws, or cardboard
white glue
crayons, different colors
stone
heavy cardboard

Optional: assorted stones, artificial plants

Directions:

1. Line the inside of the box top with aluminum foil.
2. Cover the foil with soil.
3. Sprinkle the grass seed on top of the soil. Dampen the soil with water. Keep the soil moist and grass will grow within a few weeks.
4. Press the clay into the jar top and put the jar top in the box top.
5. Stick a toy or handmade ladder into the clay so it stands upright. To make the ladder, glue together the sticks or straws. You can also cut one out of heavy cardboard which may be colored with crayons. Cover the clay with soil.
6. Place a stone inside the box top. Make a cardboard cut-out of Jacob lying down. Color him in with crayons. Place the cut-out in the box top with its head resting on the stone.
7. **Optional:** Add stones and artificial plants to make the scene more realistic.

Jacob's Ladder Movie

Materials:

1 sheet construction paper, light color
ruler
pencil

scissors
notepad (any type that is bound)
white glue
colored pencils

Directions:

1. Measure and cut the construction paper to fit the cover of the notepad. Glue to hold.
2. Draw a picture of Jacob dreaming about the angels climbing up and down the ladder (figure A). Handletter the title *Jacob's Ladder*.
3. Using one page per picture, copy the pictures in figure B or make up your own. Enlarge the pictures in figure B, if necessary, to fit the size of your notepad. Be sure to carry over the action from one picture to the next.

   Optional: To color the pictures on the pages and on the cover, dip the tips of the pencils in water to produce the effect of paint.
4. To make the pictures "move," flip the pages of the book with your thumb (figure C).

A

C

B

page 1 page 2 page 3 page 4 page 5

page 6 page 7 page 8 page 9 page 10

page 11 page 12 page 13 page 14

page 16 page 17 page 18 page 19 page 20

page 21

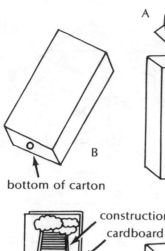

B

bottom of carton

construction paper

cardboard

D

C

← dowel

F

E

ladder glued or taped to back of carton

G

The Angels Climb the Ladder

Materials:

1 ½-gallon (2-litre) empty milk carton

scissors

1 sheet 8″ x 16″ (20.3 cm. x 40.6 cm.) construction paper, any color

white glue

pencil

crayons, paint and brush, or felt-tip marking pens, different colors

1 sheet 4″ x 11″ (2.5 cm. x 10 cm. x 28 cm.) yellow construction paper

1 4″ x 11″ (10 cm. x 28 cm.) cardboard

1 small poster board, white

1 2″ (5 cm.) long, thin dowel (home supply center, lumberyard, hardware store)

Optional: masking tape

Directions:

1. Cut the top off the milk carton (figure A).
2. Using the scissors, poke a hole in the center of the bottom of the carton (figure B).
3. Wrap the 8″ x 16″ (20.3 cm. x 40.6 cm.) paper around the carton and glue to hold.
4. Using the pencil, draw a picture of Jacob on the carton (figure C). Using the crayons, paints or marking pens, color the picture.
5. Place the 4″ x 11″ (10 cm. x 28 cm.) yellow construction paper on the 4″ x 11″ (10 cm. x 28 cm.) cardboard and glue to hold.
6. On the yellow construction paper, draw a picture of a ladder going into clouds (figure D). Color the picture.
7. Glue or tape the bottom of the picture of the ladder to the side of the carton opposite the figure of Jacob (figure E).
8. Cut three 2½″ x 4″ (6.4 cm. x 10 cm.) pieces from the poster board. On each piece, draw an angel. Color the angels, if you wish, and cut them out. Glue each angel to the dowel (figure F).
9. Stick the dowel through the hole inside the container until all the angels are hidden in the container.
10. To make the angels rise up and down the ladder, push the dowel up and down from the bottom (figure G).

Joseph and His Coat of Many Colors

Joseph was one of Jacob's twelve sons. Since Joseph was born to his mother, Rachel, and Jacob when Jacob was an old man, Jacob loved Joseph more than his other sons. To show his love, Jacob made him a coat of many colors. This made Joseph's brothers jealous, and they stopped talking to him. But they became even more jealous when Joseph had two dreams. The dreams suggested that one day Joseph's mother, father, and brothers would bow down to him. Since Joseph's brothers were afraid this might happen, they threw Joseph in a pit and stole his coat of many colors. Then they sold Joseph as a slave to the Ishmaelites who lived in Egypt. Joseph's brothers covered up their crime by smearing goat's blood on Joseph's beautiful coat and giving it to their father. Jacob, seeing the coat, assumed that Joseph must have been killed by a wild animal.

While Joseph lived with the Ishmaelites, he had many dreams that came true. When the Pharaoh (king) had two dreams that he didn't understand, he asked Joseph to come and explain them to him. Joseph told the Pharaoh that his dreams showed Egypt would have seven good years followed by seven bad years. Joseph's wisdom prompted the Pharaoh to make him second in command.

Later, when the Pharaoh's dreams came true, Joseph's brothers journeyed to Egypt during the bad years to get food. Joseph decided to forgive them, and the Pharaoh had Joseph move his father and brothers to the best part of Egypt, a region called Goshen. There Joseph took care of his family so that they would not be poor.

Now that we understand a little more about this earlier generation, let us allow our feelings to flow as we develop projects about Joseph's family and his famous coat of many colors.

Coats of Many Colors

WALLPAPER-PATCHED COAT

Cut holes large enough for a child's head and arms to go through in a large paper bag, open side down. Using pinking shears, cut out patches of wallpaper from discontinued books (free from many wallpaper stores). Glue the patches to the bag.

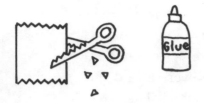

wallpaper-patched coat

IRON-ON PATCH COAT

With scissors or pinking shears, cut shapes out of assorted colored patches of iron-on tape. Arrange the shapes on an old, large shirt. Press into place with a warm iron according to the directions on the tape package.

PAINTED COAT

After placing newspapers on your work surface, take a pencil and draw different shapes on a large, unpatterned, old bath towel. Color in the design with permanent felt-tip marking pens, acrylic paints or liquid embroidery. Wear the coat like a cloak around your shoulders.

STENCILLED COAT

Make a stencil by drawing a shape on the inside of a box top and cutting it out. Place the stencil on an old, unpatterned bathrobe. Using fabric spray paint (craft store), lightly spray over the cut-out hole. Carefully lift off the stencil. Repeat the design by wiping the ink from the stencil, placing it on another area of the bathrobe and spraying again. You might want to use different colors. Let dry.

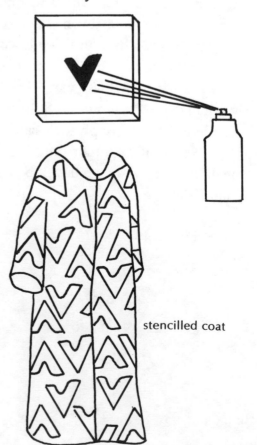

iron-on patch coat

stencilled coat

painted coat

Batiked Coat of Many Colors

Materials:

large pillowcase, unpatterned
scissors
pencil
paper
newspapers
paraffin wax (food or craft store)
old electric frying pan or hot plate, tin can and pan or double boiler

candy thermometer
wide brush
fine brush
cold-water batik dye, any color (craft store)
large container or work sink
stick
iron

Optional: needle and thread, same color as pillowcase, ruler, rubber gloves, apron

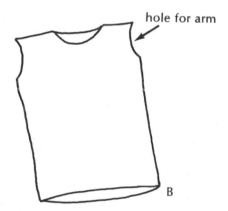

hole for head

pillowcase

A

Directions:

1. If the pillowcase is new, wash it to remove any sizing. Let dry.
2. Cut a hole in the end (seamed side) of the pillowcase large enough for your head to fit through (figure A).
3. Cut a hole in each side of the pillowcase, large enough for your arms to fit through (figure B).
4. Make a cut going up through the center of the pillowcase (figure C).
5. **Optional:** Hem the cut sides.
6. With the pencil, sketch a design on the paper. Use a ruler for drawing stripes.
7. Lightly redraw the design on the pillowcase.
8. Place several layers of newspaper on your work surface. Spread out the pillowcase on the newspaper. (Since it will be painted with wax that will seep through the material, be sure the pillowcase is in a single layer.)
9. Melt the wax in the frying pan over low heat, or put it in a can resting in a pot of water on a hot plate. CAUTION: Never melt wax in a pan directly over fire; if wax gets too hot it will burn. Use a candy thermometer to check the temperature of the wax. It should melt at not less than 170°F. (76°C) nor more than 200°F. (93°C). If the wax ignites, turn off the heat. Place a metal cover on the pan or smother the flame with baking soda. *Also ask an adult's permission before using the stove.*
10. Using the wide brush for broad areas and the fine brush for detail, "paint" the design with melted wax. The wax-coated areas will remain free from dye. Check the back of the cloth to be sure the wax has penetrated it. Since the brush can no longer be used for painting, keep it as a "wax brush" for other batik projects.

hole for arm

B

C

11. Mix the dye in the container or work sink with a stick, according to manufacturer directions. (Wear rubber gloves to protect your hands from dye and an apron to protect your clothes.) Soak the material in the dye mixture for about 45 minutes (or according to manufacturer directions). Remove and let drip dry.

12. Crumple the material to crack the wax. This will allow the dye to seep into the cracks in the wax.

13. Place the material between two sheets of newspaper. Iron, at a low setting, back and forth across the paper so that it absorbs the wax. Change the paper often until no more wax comes off.

melted wax

dye bath

Cut-Out Dolls of Joseph and His Brothers

Materials:

1 36″ x 7″ (90 cm. x 18 cm.) sheet of unpatterned paper or a large brown paper bag cut to this size
pencil
ruler

scissors
felt-tip marking pen, black
scraps of yarn or ribbon
white glue

Optional: felt-tip marking pens, different colors

Directions:

1. Measure the 36″- (90 cm.-) wide paper into twelve equal sections. Mark them by eleven ruled lines. Fold the paper on the lines, accordion style.
2. On the first section, draw a picture of Joseph wearing his coat of many colors.
3. Stack the sections (figure A). Cut out Joseph, cutting through all the layers of paper. Be careful not to cut through the folds.
4. Using the pencil, make each of the eleven plain "figures" into a brother wearing an ordinary robe.
5. Trace around all the pencil lines with the marking pen.
6. Decorate Joseph's coat by gluing on scraps of yarn or ribbon. **Optional:** Decorate Joseph's coat using marking pens in different colors.

A

Appliquéd Coat of Many Colors

Materials:

old small tablecloth, unpatterned or small sheet, unpatterned, any color
scissors
scrap paper
pencil
heavy paper or thin cardboard
small pieces of patterned and solid-color fabrics

straight pins
embroidery needle
embroidery floss or heavy-duty thread, any color
cord, long enough to make a tie belt

Optional: thin leather, felt, embroidery hoop, iron-on material that fuses fabric together with heat (fabric store)

Directions:

1. Cut a hole in the center of the tablecloth or sheet, large enough for your head to fit through.
2. Using a pencil and scrap paper, draw an undetailed design that can easily be cut apart (figure A).
3. To make patterns for the appliqués, draw each part of the design on separate pieces of heavy paper. Cut out each shape (figure B).

paper or cardboard

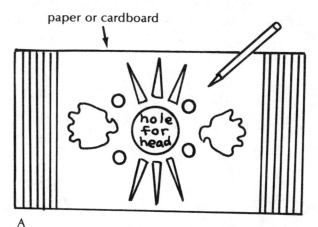

A

B

4. Arrange the patterns in a pretty design on the various pieces of fabric. Experiment with combinations of colors and patterns. Pin each pattern to the selected material (figure C).

5. Leave about one-half inch (1.3 cm.) for a hem around the patterns and cut them out (figure D). If using material that does not unravel, such as felt or leather, there is no need to allow for a hem. So that the material can be hemmed neatly, cut notches into the edges of any rounded design (figure E). Remove pins.

6. Turn under the edges of each cut-out one-half inch (1.3 cm.) and pin them to the background material used in step 1 according to the design you made in step 4.

7. With embroidery floss and a needle, appliqué or sew the pinned fabric pieces to the background material using a buttonhole stitch (figure F). To prevent the material from puckering, keep the material as flat as possible while sewing, or use an embroidery hoop. Because the inside of the coat is not lined, the stitches that show should be neat. Remove pins.

buttonhole stitch

F

fabric

pinned pattern

C

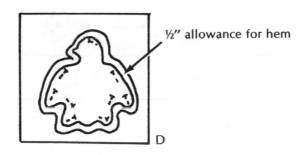

½" allowance for hem

D

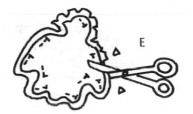

E

62

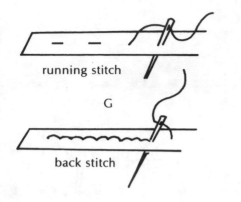

running stitch

G

back stitch

If you prefer not to have the stitches show, hem each part of the fabric cut-outs. Pin the hemmed cut-outs to pieces of iron-on material. Trace around the cut-outs. Remove the pins and cut out the iron-on designs underneath. Place the iron-on designs on the background fabric used in step 1. Place the matching parts of the fabric cut-outs on top of them. Set a steam iron at "wool" setting, and iron each part of the cut-out for a few seconds. As the iron-on material melts underneath, the cut-outs will stick to the background material.

8. **Optional:** Use a running stitch or back stitch to add detail to the appliqué (figure G).

9. Make a belt by tying a cord around your waist.

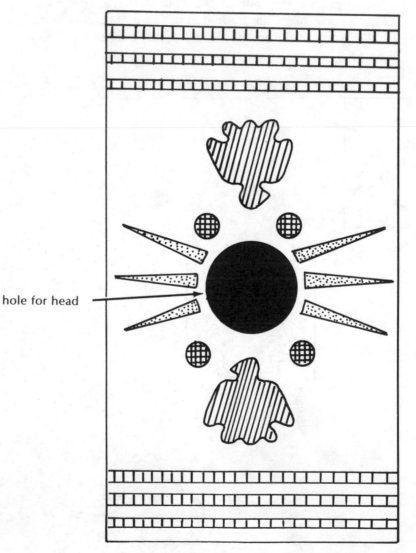

hole for head

The Twelve Tribes

Jacob was Isaac's son and Abraham's grandson. His strength of character inspired God to change his name from Jacob to Israel, meaning "he who strives with God." Jacob had twelve sons whose descendants called themselves Israelites, or the children of Israel. They separated into twelve tribes named after Jacob's sons. The land of Canaan was divided, and each portion was settled by a different tribe. Each tribe is known by a special sign or symbol.

Reuben	mandrake plant	Joseph	sheaf of grain
Simeon	city-gate of Shechem	Benjamin	wolf
Levi	High Priest and breastplate	Dan	serpent
Judah	lion	Naphtali	female deer
Issachar	donkey	Gad	tent
Zebulun	ship	Asher	olive tree

Making the symbols of the twelve tribes reminds us of the humble origin of the Israelite people.

Painted Eggs of the Twelve Tribes in a Carton

Materials:

a dozen eggs
pin or needle
bowl
pencil
fine tip felt marking pens, different colors

egg carton
1 sheet of drawing paper, 8½" x 11" (215 mm. x 279 mm.)
ruler
scissors
white glue

Directions:

1. Remove the contents from each eggshell by "blowing" them out. To "blow," shake the egg to loosen the inside. Using a pin or needle, poke a hole in both ends of the egg. Wiggle the pin to enlarge one hole slightly. Hold the egg over the bowl so the end with the small hole is on top. Blow through the small hole until the contents drip into the bowl through the larger hole on the bottom. To clean the inside of the shell, drip water into the larger hole, shake the shell, and blow out the water. Let dry.
2. Using the pencil, draw a symbol representing each of the twelve tribes on each of the twelve shells.
3. Using the marking pens, color each of the symbols.
4. Measure and cut a piece of paper to fit the inside lid of the egg carton. Lightly rule twelve lines on the paper. Using a marking pen, write facts about the twelve tribes. Refer to the symbols mentioned in the introduction. Let dry. Carefully erase the ruled lines. Glue the paper to the inside of the lid.
5. To display, place each egg in the carton and leave the lid open.

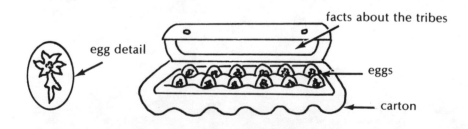

egg detail

facts about the tribes

eggs

carton

Paper Mosaic of the Tribes of Israel

Reuben

Materials:

1 large poster board, about 12″ x 18″ (30.5 cm. x 46 cm.), any color
pencil

sample paint charts or colored paper, different colors
scissors
white glue
glue-on picture hanger

Directions:

1. With the pencil, trace the symbols shown below, or draw your own, on the poster board.
2. Cut the sample paint charts or colored paper into small odd-shaped pieces. Arrange them on your drawing, leaving small spaces between each piece.
3. When you are satisfied with the pattern, glue the pieces down one by one. Let dry.
4. Glue the picture hanger to the back of the poster board and hang.

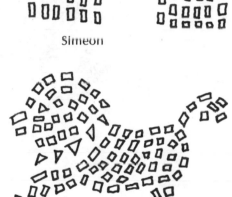

Simeon

Levi

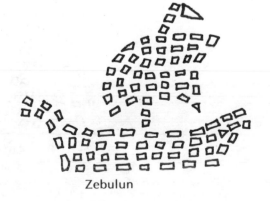

Judah

Issachar

Zebulun

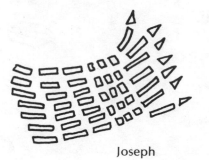

Joseph

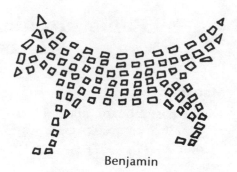

Benjamin

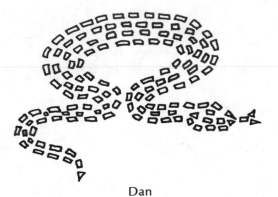

Dan

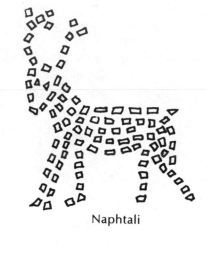

Naphtali

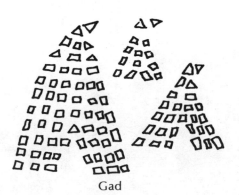

Gad

Asher

Silhouette "Photograph" of the Twelve Tribes

Materials:

pencil

construction paper, any color

scissors

any magazine or book larger than the photographic paper

photographic paper (use outdated paper as it is much less expensive—available in camera stores) or blueprint paper

1 pan of fixative (camera store)

1 pan of water

tongs

paper towels

poster board, several inches larger than the photographic paper

white glue

glue-on picture hanger

Directions:

1. With the pencil, draw silhouette symbols of each of the twelve tribes on the construction paper and cut out.

2. In a darkened room, open the magazine or book and place a sheet of the photographic paper on top of an inside page. Arrange the cut-out symbols on the photographic paper and close the book or magazine.

3. Take the closed book out into the sunlight. Open the book and expose the light-sensitive photographic paper, with the arranged symbols, to the sunlight. In less than five minutes, the paper around the cutouts should darken. To stop the darkening process, close the book. Return to the darkened room and remove the cut-outs.

4. Mix the fixative according to package directions. Place the photographic paper in the fixative solution for a few minutes. This will help prevent the color from fading.

5. With the tongs, carefully remove the picture and place it in the pan of water for a few minutes. Remove the picture and blot between paper towels. Let dry.

6. Center the picture on the poster board and glue to hold. Glue the picture hanger to the back of the posterboard and hang.

Moses

Moses' mother was named Jocheved and his father was named Amram. Miriam was his sister and Aaron was his brother. They lived in Egypt where the Pharaoh had condemned the Hebrews to slavery. He wanted to keep them from gaining power and siding with his enemies. He also tried to reduce their numbers by ordering their newborn sons to be killed. When Moses was only three months old, Miriam placed him in a basket and hid him in the bulrushes along the Nile. He was rescued by the Pharaoh's daughter. She raised him in the palace and gave him his name, Moses, meaning "I drew him out of the water." Moses never forgot his Hebrew background.

God spoke to Moses through a burning bush and commanded him to lead his people out of slavery in Egypt and into Canaan, the Promised Land. When the Pharaoh would not let Moses do this, God made the Egyptians suffer through ten plagues. Finally, the Pharaoh agreed to let the Israelites go free. Moses led them to safety across the Red Sea, which God parted to let them through. He made it come together again when the Egyptians tried to catch the Israelites, and the Egyptian soldiers drowned.

Moses brought the twelve loosely organized Israelite tribes together. Through this great prophet, God gave the Hebrews His laws. With the help of God, Moses guided the people through the hardships inflicted upon them by their enemies.

When Jewish people retell the story of Moses on Passover, they remember their days of slavery and celebrate their freedom. As we become filled with the spirit of Moses and his people, it will be easy to add our personal touch to each project.

Spoon and Cup of Moses and the Burning Bush

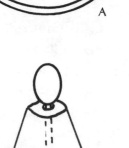

Materials:

2 paper cups (refills for plastic coffee-cup holders or pointed cups for dispensers)
1 plastic spoon
scissors

felt-tip marking pens, black and red
cotton
white construction paper
white glue
twig from tree or a stick

Directions:

1. To make Moses' body, turn the cup upside down. Cut a hole in the center of the top of the cup (figure A).
2. Insert the spoon, bowl side up, through the hole in the cup. If the spoon handle is too long, break off a piece of it so that the bowl rests on top of the cup (figure B).
3. With the black marking pen, draw a face on the rounded side of the spoon head. Draw sleeves on the sides of the cup (figure C).
4. Glue on cotton eyebrows and a cotton beard and mustache (figure D).
5. Cut little hands from the construction paper. Glue one hand next to one sleeve. To make Moses holding his staff, glue the other hand around the twig. Glue this hand to the other sleeve (figure E).
6. To make the burning bush, turn the remaining cup upside down. Make jagged cuts in the cup as shown in figure F. Use the red marking pen to color the "bush."

A

B

C

D

E

F   burning bush

Baby Moses in a Basket
in the River Nile

spoon

thread tie

material

A

Materials:

1 small wooden ice cream spoon

colorful swatch of material or print handkerchief

thread, color to match material or handkerchief

black felt-tip marking pen, fine point

the slide-out part of a large kitchen-size matchbox

household aluminum foil

1 empty tin-foil pie pan

cotton

small weighted plastic plants (such as for a fish tank—pet store)

Optional: needle

Directions:

1. To make the "baby," wrap the material around the spoon, leaving the rounded side of the bowl of the spoon exposed. To hold the material in place, tie thread around the neck of the spoon. Wrap the rest of the material around the "body" of the spoon (figure A). Optional: Secure the open ends of the material with needle and thread.

2. With the marking pen, draw eyes, a nose, and a mouth on the exposed part of the spoon. Draw strands of hair coming out from under the cloth wrapping (figure B).

3. To make the matchbox waterproof, cover it with foil.

4. Pad the inside of the matchbox with cotton.

5. Place baby Moses in the matchbox basket.

6. Fill the pie tin half way up with water.

7. Place the basket in the "river."

8. Arrange the plastic plants around the basket.

B

Moses

cotton padding

matchbox

water

pie tin

A

B

The Red Sea Parts for Moses and the Israelites

Materials:

pipe cleaners (tobacco shop, variety store)
facial tissue
yarn, different colors
fine black felt-tip marking pen
fine red felt-tip marking pen
cotton
wooden beads (craft store)
twig

white glue
cardboard, 1½″ (4 cm.) square
black yarn
scissors
1 shoe box
blue paint, acrylic
paintbrush
sand

Optional: shells, fish cut-outs from construction paper

Directions:

1. Decide how many pipe-cleaner figures you want to make. You'll need two pipe cleaners for each figure.
2. To form a figure, bend two pipe cleaners in half. Join the two pipe cleaners as shown in figure A.
3. Twist one half of the top pipe cleaner as shown in figure B.
4. Bend the untwisted portions of the twisted pipe cleaner to form a neck and arms (figure C).
5. Bend each tip of the pipe cleaner arms to form hands. Bend each tip of the pipe cleaner legs to form feet (figure D).
6. To make a robe, push the neck of the pipe cleaner up through the center of a facial tissue. Gather the folds of the tissue around the arms and body and secure at the waist with a piece of yarn (figure E).
7. To make a head, push the neck of the pipe cleaner up through the hole in a bead. Using the black marking pen, draw eyes and a nose. Using the red marking pen, draw a mouth (figure F).

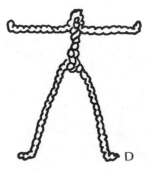

C

D

E

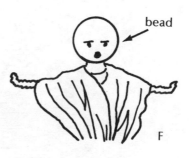

bead

F

8. To turn the lead figure (see figure K) into Moses, glue cotton hair and a cotton beard to a bead head. To make a staff, bend one hand around the twig.

9. To make hair for the rest of the figures, wind yarn around the square of cardboard twelve times (figure G). Tie the top strands together (figure H). Cut apart the bottom strands (figure I). Glue the hair to the bead head.

10. To form the parting of the Red Sea, cut off both narrow ends of the shoe box. Cut each side to look like waves (figure J).

11. Paint both sides of the "waves" blue.

12. Arrange the pipe cleaner figures in a row going down the center of the shoe box. Glue the feet to hold (figure K).

13. To make the bottom of the box look like the floor of the sea, spread a fine coat of glue on it. Before the glue hardens, sprinkle it with sand. **Optional:** Add shells and paper cut-outs of fish. When the glue is dry, gently brush off the excess sand.

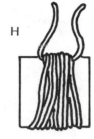

G

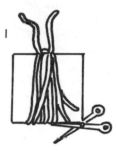

H

I

J

K

Moses and the Ten Plagues

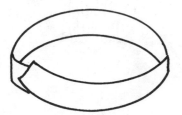

Materials:

construction paper 2″ x 18″ (5 cm. x 47 cm.), any color
pencil
ruler
scissors

10 pieces of construction paper, 1½″ (4 cm.) square, light colors
fine black felt-tip marking pen
poster board 3″ x 10″ (7.6 cm. x 25.4 cm.), white

Directions:

1. Slightly overlap the ends of the construction paper strip to make a circle. Glue to hold. Cut slits all around the circle, 1¾″ apart (figure A).
2. Using the marking pen, write a different plague, in the order in which they came, on each of the ten pieces of construction paper. Turn the paper over and print the same plague on the back of each piece. Insert a paper in each slit of the circle (figure B).

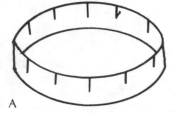

A

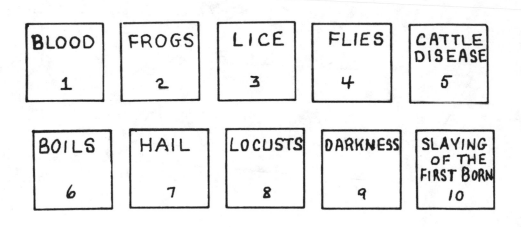

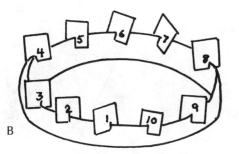

B

3. Fold the poster board in half, so that each side measures 3″ x 5″ (3.8 cm. x 12.7 cm.). On one side of the poster board, take the pencil and draw a picture of Moses. Cut around the outline of the figure, going through both pieces of poster board. Take care not to cut through the fold on top of the poster board (figure C).

4. Using the marking pen, trace around the pencil lines of Moses.

5. Turn the poster board cut-out over, and draw a picture of the Pharaoh on the other side. Using the marking pen, trace around the pencil lines (figure D).

6. Place the figures of Moses and the Pharaoh in the center of the ring (figure E).

Moses

C

E

Pharaoh

D

Crewel Painting of Moses and the Burning Bush

Materials:

1 sheet drawing paper, 9" x 24" (23 cm. x 61 cm.) or less
pencil
dressmaker's carbon (fabric store or variety store)
linen material, 10" x 25" (25.4 cm. x 63.5 cm.)
cotton batting (fabric store)
white craft cement
yarn (black, white, red)

wide-eyed embroidery needle
2 pieces of plywood, 1 9" x 24" (23 cm. x 61 cm.) and 1 16" x 30" (40.5 cm. x 76 cm.) (lumberyard or home supply store)
staple gun
black felt, 18" x 32" (46 cm. x 81 cm.)
glue-on picture hanger

Directions:

1. Enlarge the picture shown to fit the 9" x 24" (23 cm. x 61 cm.) piece of wood, or sketch one of your own design on the drawing paper. Transfer the drawing by placing the carbon face down on the linen. Place the drawing of Moses face up on the carbon and trace around the lines. The picture should show on the linen.

2. Using the white craft cement, glue cotton batting to the drawing of Moses on the linen. Glue a tiny section at a time. Sew over it with straight stitch (figure A). Continue using the straight stitch until the entire figure of Moses is sewn with yarn. Create a dimensional effect by not padding the flames around Moses. Use the stitch (figure B) to fill in the flames.

3. Center the completed picture on the 9" x 24" (23 cm. x 61 cm.) wood. Wrap the excess linen around the back of the board, stretching tightly, and secure with staple gun.

4. Wrap the black felt around the 16" x 30" (40.5 cm. x 76 cm.) board, stapling the excess material to the back.

5. Center the embroidered, linen-covered board on the black felt. Glue to hold (figure C). Let dry.

6. To hang, attach picture hanger to back of board.

Straight stitch goes from side to side over the cotton batting.

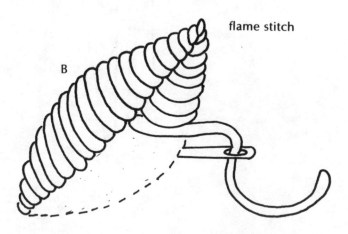

flame stitch

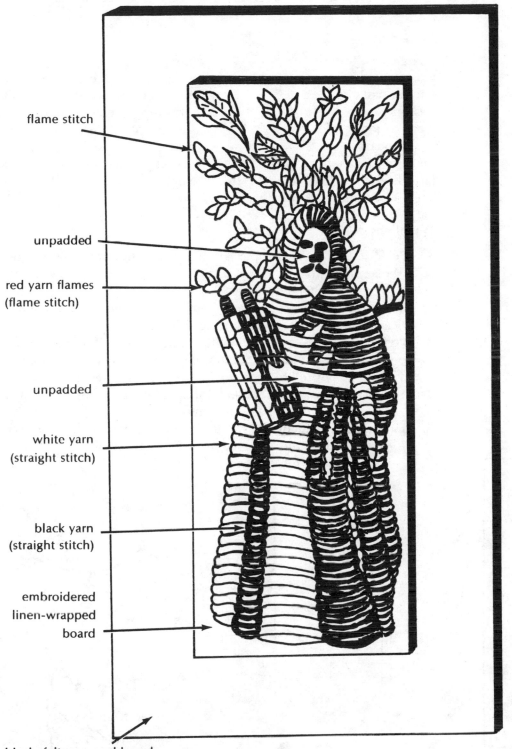

flame stitch

unpadded

red yarn flames
(flame stitch)

unpadded

white yarn
(straight stitch)

black yarn
(straight stitch)

embroidered
linen-wrapped
board

black, felt-wrapped board

Shoe Box and Material Moses

Materials:

2 large shoe boxes
masking tape
1 toilet-tissue roll
scissors
2 empty towel rolls
poster board
black felt-tip marking pen
large Styrofoam ball, about 4″ (10 cm.) in diameter (craft store)

white glue
cotton batting (fabric store)
cotton sheeting or muslin, white or appropriate pattern, i.e., stripe (fabric store)
wheat paste, mixed according to package directions and thinned slightly (craft store, hardware store)

Directions:

1. To form the body, tape the box tops down in their usual position. Place the two shoe boxes end to end and tape securely together (figure A). Stand upright.
2. To make the neck, cut a 1½″ (4 cm.) circle from a toilet-tissue roll and tape to the top of the boxes (figure A).
3. To form the arms, bend each of the paper towel rolls in half. (If they split, it doesn't matter because they will be covered with fabric.) Tape a bent roll to each side of the top box (figure B).
4. To make the hands, cut two hand shapes out of the poster board and tape to the cardboard arms (figure C).
5. To make the head, draw eyes on the poster board with the marking pen. Cut them out and glue them to the Styrofoam ball. Glue on cotton batting for the beard (figure D).

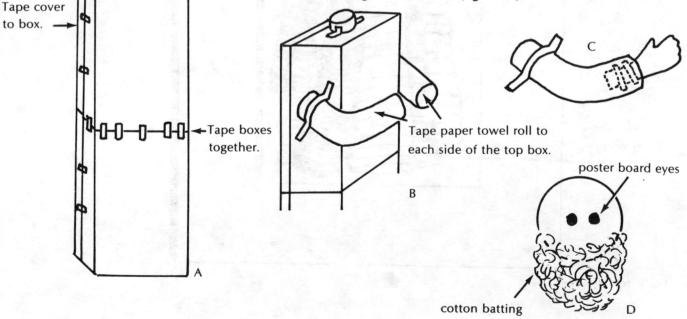

1½″ circle from toilet tissue roll. Tape to top of boxes.

Tape cover to box.

Tape boxes together.

A

Tape paper towel roll to each side of the top box.

B

C

poster board eyes

cotton batting

D

6. To make the robe, cut out a 30″ x 26″ (76 cm. x 66 cm.) piece of material, dip it into the paste mixture, run it through your fingers to remove the excess, and drape it around the neck and shoulders and the body, arranging the folds as you go.

7. To make the sleeves, cut out two 8″ x 10″ (20 cm. x 25 cm.) pieces of material. Repeat step six, but drape them around each shoulder and arm, arranging the folds as you go. Cut a 20″ x 36″ (51 cm. x 91 cm.) piece of material, treat as above, and drape over the right arm, across the back, under the left arm and down the body. Cut a 20″ x 36″ (51 cm. x 91 cm.) piece of material, treat as above, and drape over the left arm, across the back, under the right arm and down the body.

8. Glue the head to the body. Use a 10″ x 15″ (25 cm. x 38 cm.) treated piece of material to drape around the head and shoulders. Let dry.

9. Draw the shape of the tablets of the Ten Commandments on poster board, cut out and glue to hands.

The Ten Commandments

Moses led the Israelites out of Egypt and away from slavery. He led them through the wilderness to Canaan, the land of milk and honey. During the journey, the Israelites stopped and camped in the Sinai desert at the foot of a mountain. God spoke to Moses from "Mount Sinai," saying if the people obeyed Him, they would become a holy nation.

The Israelites then prepared themselves to meet with God, but when they saw the mountain smoking, and saw thunder and lightning, and heard the sound of a trumpet, they were scared. They asked Moses to speak with God instead.

The people waited at the foot of Mount Sinai, while Moses drew near the thick darkness where God was. God wrote His laws on two tablets of stone called the Ten Commandments. God gave them to Moses at the top of the mountain, telling him to deliver them to the Israelites. God also gave Moses other instructions, including how the Israelites should build an ark or chest to house His laws and commandments.

Because Moses was up on the mountain for forty days and nights, the Israelites thought he had disappeared. While they were waiting, they made a golden calf and worshiped it. When Moses returned, he was so angry that he threw down the tablets of the law, and they broke. Then he destroyed the golden calf and had the Israelites killed who had worshiped it.

God was also furious and punished the people by causing a plague. Then God renewed His special agreement with the Israelites, telling Moses to cut two stone tablets like the ones he had broken. God would rewrite His words on them. The people were to keep His commandments and worship Him according to His laws.

The Israelites carried the ark containing the laws before them as they traveled out of the desert.

We should think about God's love and forgiveness for the Israelites as we prepare the crafts in this chapter.

Mock Stone Tablets

Materials:

newspapers
cardboard, 9″ x 15″ (23 cm. x 38 cm.)
scissors
tempera or acrylic paint, gray, blue, yellow, white
sponge (or crumpled sheet of newspaper)
poster board, 12″ x 18″ (30.5 cm. x 46 cm.)

white glue
paintbrush
10 babyfood jar lids (or lids of similar size)
paper (typing, drawing)
pencil
black felt-tip marking pen
glue-on picture hanger

Directions:

1. Cover your work surface with newspapers.
2. Cut the cardboard into the shape of two adjoining tablets. Place the tablets on the paper.
3. To make the tablets look like they're made of stone, sponge their surface with gray paint. Let dry.
4. Glue the tablets to the poster board.
5. Paint clouds (white), sky (blue) and lightning (yellow) around the tablets on the poster board. Wash out the brush. Let the paint dry.
6. Place a jar lid on the drawing paper, and trace around it with the pencil. Cut out. Repeat nine more times.
7. Starting with the first letter of the Hebrew alphabet, print a letter on each circle with the marking pen. The first ten letters of the Hebrew alphabet are often used instead of words. The Hebrew numbers 1 to 10 are represented by these letters. Push a paper circle into each lid.
8. Arrange the lids on the cardboard so that the Commandments are in the proper order (five on each side) and glue to hold.
9. Attach the picture hanger and hang.

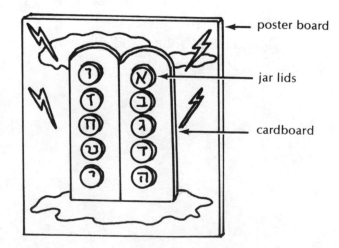

Slate Painting

Materials:

newspapers
1 piece slate (home supply center,
   lumberyard)
paper towels

chalk, any light color
acrylic paint, metallic colors
paintbrush
jar of water

Directions:

1. Cover your work surface with newspapers. Place the slate on the papers. Using paper towels, wipe the surface of the slate clean.
2. Take the chalk and draw the letters of the Hebrew alphabet on the slate, as shown in the illustration. If you make an error, erase the chalk by rubbing it with a paper towel.
3. Paint each letter. Clean your brush in water before using another color. If more than one coat of paint is necessary, let the paint dry before applying a second coat. Let dry.
4. To display, set the slate on a shelf, leaning against a wall.

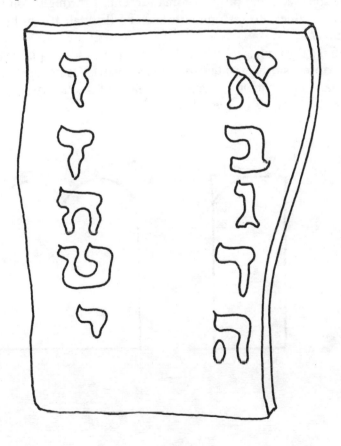

"Parchment" Window Hanging

Materials:

1 sheet typing paper
pencil
scissors
paper towels
cooking or salad oil

black ink, paint, or black permanent felt-tip marking pens
gray chalk
cellophane tape

Directions:

1. Fold the paper in half vertically. Using the whole paper, draw the rounded top of one of the tablets. Cut out, going through both halves of the paper, and unfold (figure A).
2. Place a double layer of paper towels on your work surface. Center the paper tablets on the towels.
3. Crumple a sheet of paper towel and wet it with the oil. Coat both sides of the tablets with oil. Wipe off the excess.
4. Let the oiled tablets dry on the paper towels (one or two days).
5. With the black ink, print Commandments 1 through 5 on the right-hand tablet. Print Commandments 6 through 10 on the lefthand tablet.
6. To make the tablets look like they're made of stone, place them on a textured surface (sidewalk, stucco wall). Using the side of the chalk, lightly color the entire surface of the tablets.
7. Tape the hanging to a window.

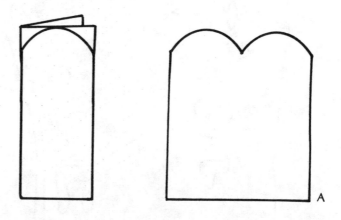

YOU SHALL NOT KILL.

YOU SHALL NOT BE
UNFAITHFUL TO YOUR
WIFE OR HUSBAND.

YOU SHALL NOT STEAL.

YOU SHALL NOT LIE.

YOU SHALL NOT COVET
(WANT) ANYTHING THAT
BELONGS TO YOUR
NEIGHBOR.

YOU SHALL HAVE NO
OTHER GOD BUT ME.

YOU SHALL NOT MAKE
ANY IMAGE OF GOD.

YOU SHALL NOT TAKE
THE NAME OF GOD IN
VAIN.

REMEMBER THE
SABBATH DAY AND
KEEP IT HOLY.

HONOR YOUR FATHER
AND YOUR MOTHER.

Israelites Enter Canaan

While Moses and the Israelites were in the wilderness, Moses sent twelve scouts ahead to find out what the area and people in Canaan were like. Each of the twelve scouts was a member of a different Israelite tribe. Moses asked them to bring back some fruit.

The scouts reported that the land was so bountiful that it flowed with milk and honey. They also told stories of giants who lived there. The Israelites were afraid. Because of their lack of faith, God made them wander in the desert for forty years. Then the Lord chose Joshua to lead the Israelites safely across the River Jordan into Canaan.

Every tribe except the Levites, who handled the religious affairs for the other tribes, received a portion of Canaan. The Levites spread themselves among the others in order to teach the word of God.

Let us try to follow in the footsteps of these ancient people, as we express ourselves creatively.

Sculptured Soap

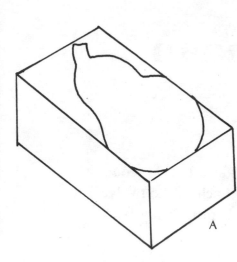

A

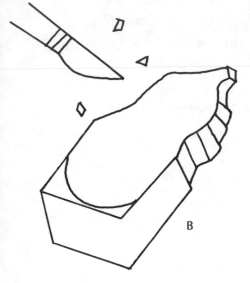

B

Materials:

1 large cake of soap	saucepan
newspapers	stick for stirring
penknife or kitchen knife	watercolor paint
pencil	paintbrush
pointed stick, nail file, pin or comb	miniature wicker basket (craft store)

Directions:

1. Start with soap that is fresh, not dried out. To soften, unwrap the bar and allow it to stand at room temperature overnight.
2. Cover a work surface with newspapers.
3. If there's lettering on the soap, scrape it off with the knife.
4. With the pencil, draw an outline of a piece of fruit on the soap (figure A).
5. With the knife, whittle the soap slowly, while looking at a real piece of fruit, if available, until you have copied the shape as closely as possible (figure B). Take the pointed stick and add marks for texture (figure C). Note: If part of the carved soap breaks, mend it by putting the soap scrapings in a pan containing one-half inch (1.3 cm.) of water. Place the saucepan on a burner over low heat and stir with a stick until the mixture looks like pudding. With the stick, spread some of the mixture on the broken parts. Press the broken parts together and allow to set.
6. To color the sculptured soap fruit, brush on watercolor paint.
7. Repeat steps 1 through 5 to make additional pieces of fruit.
8. To display, place in the little wicker basket. **Optional:** Use as a prop in a diorama.

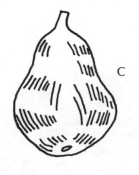

C

D

Clay and Jute Fruit

Materials:

clay, air-hardening or oven-hardening (craft store)

white glue

jute cord (craft store) or yarn, different colors

permanent felt-tip marking pen, black

platter, tray or bowl

Directions:

1. Mold the clay into several kinds of fruit (including grapes, figs, and pomegranates). Allow to air dry or "fire" (bake) in oven. If oven "fired," allow to cool. (Be sure you have an adult's permission to oven-fire.)

2. Apply white glue to a small area of one piece of fruit. Press one color of jute cord or yarn onto the glued area. Keep the strands tightly together. (**Optional:** Leave space for adding second color of jute cord to make another design.) Repeat with the other fruit. Let dry.

3. Using the marking pen, print the following words on the side of the platter, tray, or bowl.

   Be ye of good courage, and bring of
   the fruit of the land.

   These words were part of Moses' message to the Israelite scouts sent to spy on Canaan and its people.

4. Arrange the fruit on the platter, tray, or in the bowl and display.

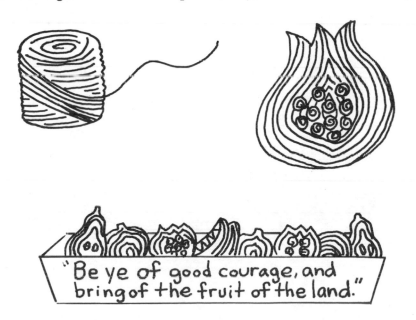

Bread and Glue Miniatures of Temple Priests Carrying the Holy Ark to Canaan

Materials:

wax paper
6 slices of white bread
bowl
white glue
measuring spoons
toothpick

thick brush
acrylic paints, different colors
fine paintbrush
clear spray sealer (craft store)
small wooden plaque or picture
    frame with backing

Optional: hand lotion

Directions:

1. Cover the work surface with wax paper.
2. To make bread-and-glue dough, tear the six slices of white bread into small pieces and place them in a bowl.
3. Add six tablespoons of white glue. Mix with a spoon and knead with your hands in the bowl until the dough is no longer sticky. If the dough is too dry, add a few more drops of glue. To make the dough easier to handle, rub hand lotion into your fingers and palms.
4. With your hands, take small balls of dough and shape it into priests and a Holy Ark. Flatten the back of each shape for mounting later on. (If you want the sculpture to be larger, double the dough recipe.)
5. Use the toothpick to make decorative marks.

6. Mix two tablespoons of white glue with two tablespoons of water. Brush the mixture on each shape. Let dry. This will prevent cracks from forming.
7. Take the fine brush and with the acrylic paints, color the sculptures. Let dry.
8. Spray with a coat of sealer. Let dry.
9. Coat the back of each piece with undiluted glue and mount on the plaque or in the frame.

Cut-Outs and Drawings of Israelites Marching Into Canaan

Materials:

1 sheet poster board, any size
magazines
scissors

glue
fine felt-tip marking pen, black
glue-on picture hanger

Optional: watercolor paints, paintbrush, jar of water

Directions:

1. Cut out an assortment of appropriate looking heads from the magazines.
2. Arrange the heads on the poster board and glue to hold.

3. Using the marking pen, draw a costumed body to go with each head. A headdress may also be added.
4. **Optional:** Color the costumes with the watercolor paints. Rinse the brush in a jar of water before switching to another color.
5. To hang, attach the glue-on hanger to the back of the picture.

Fruit-from-Canaan Painting on Plastic

Materials:

1 sheet drawing paper, 8½" x 11" (215 mm. x 279 mm.)	acrylic paints, different colors
pencil	paint brush
1 sheet clear, stiff plastic, 8½" x 11" (215 mm. x 279 mm.) (art supply store)	box
	sand (from beach or home-and-garden supply store)

Directions:

1. With the pencil, draw a picture of two Israelites carrying grapes back from Canaan. Leave plenty of room at the bottom (figure A).
2. Place the plastic over the drawing so that the edges meet.
3. Using the acrylic paints, copy the picture onto the plastic. Let dry.
4. Fill the box with sand. Insert the bottom of the plastic into the "desert" sand.

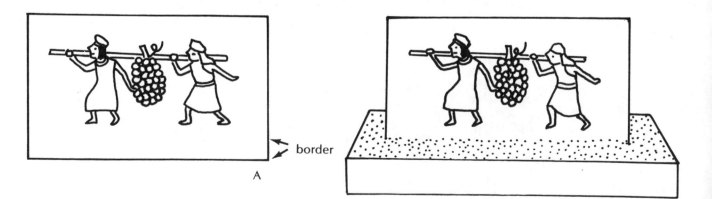

border

A

The Story of Ruth

Naomi and Elimelech and their two sons, Mahlon and Chilion, lived in Bethlehem. Because of a great famine, they moved to Moab. Elimelech died and Naomi, alone, watched her sons grow into adults.

Both of her sons married Moabites. One was named Orpah and the other was named Ruth. Before too long, Naomi's sons became ill and died. Now Orpah and Ruth were widows just like Naomi.

Naomi decided to return to her old home in Bethlehem. Orpah wished her well and said good-bye, but Ruth did not want to leave Naomi. She said, "Whither thou goest, I will go and where thou lodgest, I will lodge. Thy people shall be my people and thy God my God."

Naomi and Ruth went to live in Bethlehem. It was there that Naomi's husband had a wealthy relative, Boaz, who owned fields of grain. It was a custom for farmers to leave fallen stalks of grain for poor people. Ruth gathered the grain to be used for food.

Boaz asked about Ruth and was told that she came from the land of Moab with Naomi. To reward Ruth for her kindness to Naomi, Boaz told her she could gather grain from his fields and drink his water.

Boaz then met with Ruth's relatives and bought the land that had belonged to Elimelech. In doing this, according to custom, he also got to marry Ruth.

Ruth and Boaz had a son named Obed. Naomi became the nurse of the child who was to become the grandfather of David, second king of Israel.

As we identify with Ruth's love, we become eager to create her in various artistic mediums.

Ruth Gathering Grain in the Fields of Boaz

Materials:

1 piece white poster board, any size

permanent felt-tip marking pen, black

rubber cement in a tube

pastels or chalk, different colors

paintbrush

dish of water

1 piece colored poster board, at least 1" (2.5 cm.) larger all around than the white poster board

glue-on picture hanger

Directions:

1. Using the marking pen, draw a picture on the white poster board of Ruth gathering grain in the fields of Boaz.
2. Holding the tube of rubber cement as you would a pencil, fill in only the areas of the drawing you want to remain white. Let dry.
3. Take each pastel separately, and holding it on its side, make a broad stroke across the surface of the white poster board set apart for that color (see drawing).
4. To soften the colors, brush water over the pastelled surface. Let dry.
5. With your index finger, gently rub off the rubber cement, along with any color sticking to it, so that the surface of the poster board shows. (**Optional:** Add extra details to the drawing with the marking pen.)
6. Using rubber cement, mount the drawing on the colored poster board.
7. Attach the glue-on picture hanger and hang.

blue   green   pink   orange   yellow   rust

Wire Figure of Ruth Carrying Wheat

Materials:

white paper
pencil
colored plastic coated wire (craft store)

scissors
1 jar cover
1 sheet of plain paper, any color
white glue

Directions:

1. Using the pencil, draw a wire figure of Ruth in an action pose on the white paper (figure A).
2. Bend the wire into the shape of the figure in the drawing. Twist the wire to hold it in position (figure B). The figure should be no more than 6″ (15 cm.) high for easy handling. Use the scissors to cut away excess wire.
3. To make the wheat, cut six, 4″ (10 cm.) lengths of wire. Twist the tops (figure C).
4. Bend one of Ruth's hands around the "wheat" to hold it in place.
5. To make the base, place the jar cover on the sheet of paper and trace around it. Cut along the pencil line. Press the paper cut-out into the cover.
6. Glue the figure to the base (figure D).

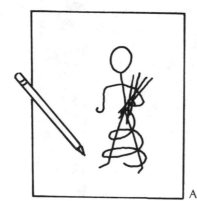

A

B

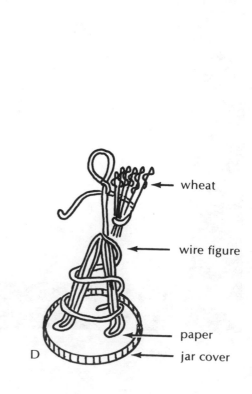

C

wheat

wire figure

paper

jar cover

D

A Ruth Bottle Doll

Materials:

1 32-ounce (1-litre) soda bottle, empty

1 Styrofoam ball, 3″ (7.5 cm.) in diameter

gesso (a primer found in craft stores)

red acrylic paint

paintbrush

small disposable container

stick

heavy black yarn

white glue

burlap, felt or linen, neutral color

ruler

pencil

scissors

2 2″ (5 cm.) squares construction paper, white

thread, color of fabric

needle

dried wheat (florist or craft store)

Directions:

1. To make Ruth's head, place the Styrofoam ball on the top of the bottle. Put gesso into the small container and, with the stick, stir in a few drops of red acrylic paint until the mixture becomes light pink. Paint the Styrofoam ball. Let dry. Set aside the paint that's left.

2. To make Ruth's hair, cut forty 30″ (76 cm.) lengths of yarn. Tie them together in the middle with another 30″ (76 cm.) length of yarn. Glue the hair to the top of the head. Separate the lengths so they fall evenly.

3. To make the top of Ruth's dress, cut out a piece of material 8″ (20.3 cm.) high by 14″ (35.6 cm.) wide. Fold the material in half as shown by the dotted line in figure A. Measure in 5″ (12.7 cm.) from both ends of folded material and 1½″ (3.8 cm.) up from bottom as shown by the dotted lines in figure B. Cut out, as shown by the shaded areas in figure B. Be sure to cut through both layers of material. Turn the material inside out to hide the pencil lines.

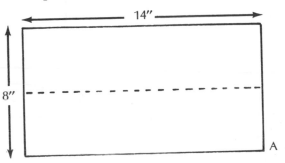

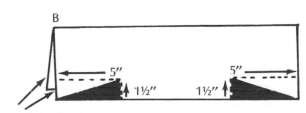

Cut through both layers of material.

4. Cut through the middle of one layer (figure C). Fit the material around the bottle (figure D). Glue to hold.
5. To make Ruth's hands, fold the corners of each 2″ square down. Fold the sides in and secure with glue (figure E).

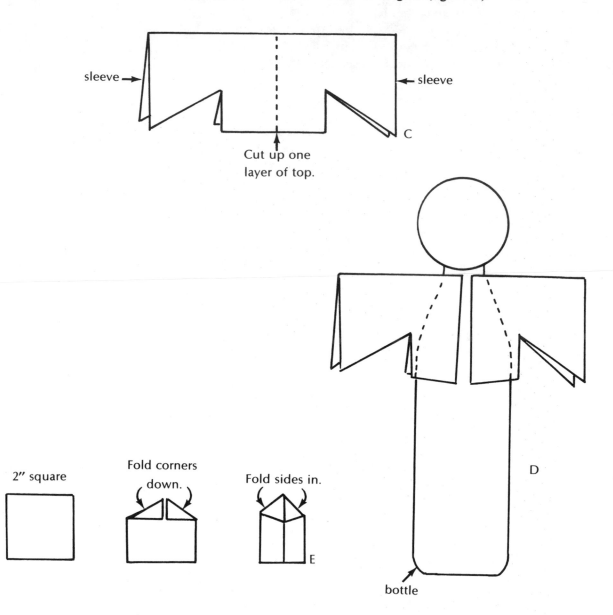

sleeve →   ← sleeve

C

Cut up one
layer of top.

D

2″ square   Fold corners
down.   Fold sides in.

E

bottle

6. Insert the ends of the "hands," seam side facing front, between folds of each sleeve and glue (figure F).

7. To make Ruth's skirt, cut out a piece of material 9″ (23 cm.) high by 18″ (46 cm.) wide. Make a running stitch through the top of the material (figure G). Pull the thread to gather the material so that it fits around the bottle, with the ends overlapping slightly. Sew the overlapping ends closed. The skirt should overlap the top of the dress. To make the belt, trim a strip off the bottom of the skirt and tie it around the gathers at the waist. This will hide the running stitch (figure H).

8. Cross the hands and sleeves across the doll's chest and glue to hold. Place the wheat between the sleeves and the body. **Optional:** Add yarn eyes and any other decorative trim desired.

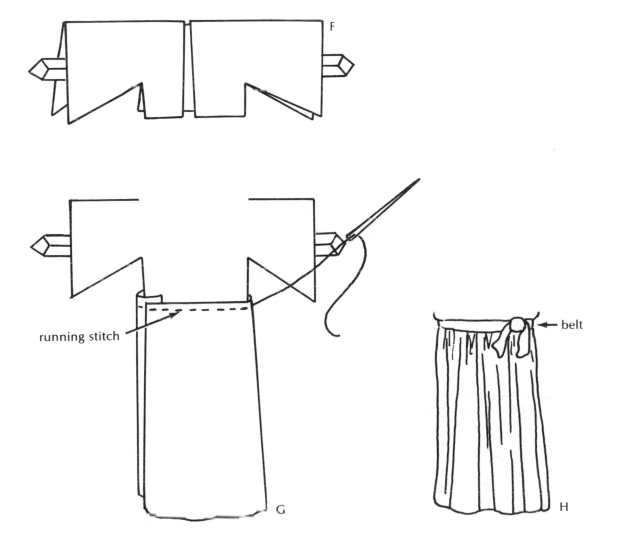

Daniel in the Lion's Den

Nebuchadnezzar became king of Babylon. He chose prisoners from the children of Israel having the best ability to learn the language and the ways of his people. These children were to be taught to serve him in the palace.

Among the chosen were Daniel, who was renamed Belteshazzar; Hananiah, who was called Shadrach; Mishael, who became known as Meshach; and Azariah, who was called Abednego.

God blessed Daniel by giving him the wisdom to understand the meaning of dreams.

With this power, Daniel explained the dreams of King Nebuchadnezzar. He also predicted the death of the king's son, Belshazzar, and the fate of his kingdom. When these prophecies came to pass, the new king, Darius, appointed Daniel to rule over Babylon. This made the other Babylonian leaders jealous.

King Darius worshiped many gods while Daniel worshiped only one God. Daniel broke the good king's law by bowing in prayer to his God. This gave the other rulers an excuse to get rid of Daniel. They persuaded the king to have Daniel thrown to the lions.

One of God's angels appeared and protected Daniel. King Darius had Daniel released from the den when he saw that he had not been harmed. The jealous rulers were punished in Daniel's place.

A new law was made commanding all Babylonians to worship Daniel's God, the God of Israel.

Our faith grows as we read about heroic ancestors like Daniel; our creativity grows as we express ourselves through craft-related projects.

102

Rising Figure Puppet of Daniel in the Lion's Den

Materials:

heavy cardboard, as large as you would like the puppet and lions to be
pencil
crayons, different colors
scissors or craft knife
string
needle

Optional: basswood or hardboard, sabre or coping saw

Directions:

1. Using the pencil, draw on the cardboard a figure of Daniel with his arms raised. Color and cut it out.
2. Cut a piece of cardboard as wide as the figure's armspread.
3. Using the pencil, draw two lions, as shown in the illustration, on the cardboard. Color and cut them out.
4. Cut a length of string, twice as long as the cardboard figure of Daniel. Thread the string through the needle, knotting the long end.
5. Sew through one end of the cardboard piece, through the center of one hand and through the head of the lion (see illustration). Knot the string.
6. Repeat step 5 for the other side.
7. To make a handle, thread the needle and knot the ends of the string together. Sew to the center of the cardboard piece as shown in figure A.
8. Hang the puppet by the loop from a doorknob or knob of a dresser.
9. To make Daniel rise from the "den of lions," pull both lions (and strings) out slightly. To lower the figure, push both lions (and strings) together.
10. **Optional:** To make a sturdier puppet, saw the figure and lions out of wood. Glue a lion cut-out to both ends of the strings.

Peek Box of Daniel in the Lion's Den

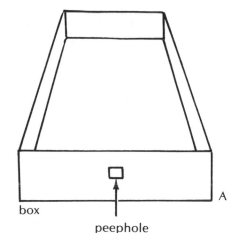

box

peephole

A

Materials:

shoe box with cover
pencil
scissors

pictures of Daniel and lions
(either from a magazine or calendar, or hand drawn and colored)
cardboard
white glue

Optional: paint, paintbrush, solid-colored paper, felt-tipped marking pen, any color

Directions:

1. **Optional:** If the shoe box is covered with a design, paint it with a solid color or glue paper to sides.
2. Cut a window just big enough to see through in one end of the box (figure A).
3. Cut a long, narrow slit down the center of the box cover for light to enter (figure B).
4. Place the picture of Daniel on the cardboard and trace around it. Draw a tab at the bottom of the drawing (figure C). Cut out the tabbed cardboard figure. Glue the figure to the cardboard. Repeat with each lion.
5. Arrange the pictures toward the rear of the box. The front of each should be facing the peep hole at the end. Glue the tabs down to hold.
6. Replace the lid. To see the scene, peek through the hole.
7. **Optional:** With the marking pen, decorate the sides with warning signs such as a *Lion's Den, Look at Your Own Risk* or *Beware of Lions.*

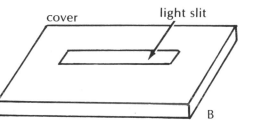

cover

light slit

B

C

tab

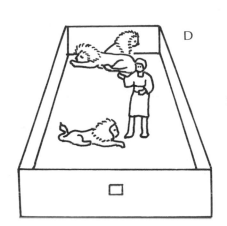

D

A No-Brush Acrylic Painting of Daniel in The Lion's Den

Materials:

picture of Daniel, cut from an old calendar or workbook

1 piece of heavy cardboard, the size of the picture

glue

acrylic paint tubes, any color (size to fit paint tip)

plastic tips that fit paint tubes for painting (art store)

glue-on picture hanger

Optional: 1 sheet drawing paper, paint brush

Directions:

1. Glue the picture on the cardboard. **Optional:** Paint your own picture on paper and glue it to the cardboard.
2. Remove the cover from a tube of paint. In its place, attach the special tip. Squeeze the tube so that paint will ooze out of the hole in the tip. "Paint" the parts of the picture that you want to highlight. (Check the instructions on the paint-tip packaging for special effects.)
3. When you have finished using a tube, replace the tip with the top. Clean the tip in warm water.
4. Let the picture dry.
5. To hang, attach the picture hanger to the back of the cardboard.

plastic paint tip

Daniel in the Lion's Den
Slide Show

Materials:

cardboard or oak tag, about 12" x 18" (30.5 cm. x 46 cm.)
pencil
ruler
scissors

felt-tip marking pens, crayons or paint, different colors
6 sheets of drawing paper, 4" x 6" (10 cm. x 15 cm.)
holepunch
paper fastener

Directions:

1. To make the theatre, measure in 5" (12.7 cm.) from each end of the cardboard and draw lines as shown in figure A. Fold along the drawn lines and unfold.
2. On the center section, draw the front of the theatre (figure B). Color the drawing.

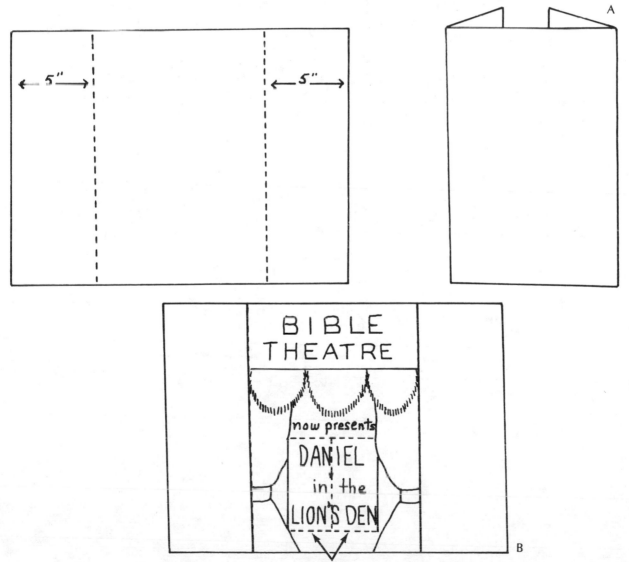

doors

3. Cut around three sides of each door as shown by the dotted lines in figure B.

4. On each sheet of 4″ x 6″ (10 cm. x 15 cm.) paper, draw a scene telling the story of Daniel (figure C). The dialogue is not drawn onto the sheets of paper. It is spoken as the show goes on. Color each scene.

5. Stack the papers in the right order, with scene #1 on top. Punch a hole through the top as shown in figure D. Push a paper fastener through the holes. Open the back of the fasteners to hold the papers in place (figure E).

6. To put on a show, fold back the end sections of the theatre so it can stand. Stand behind the theatre. Open the doors exposing page one. Slide page one up, exposing page two behind it. Describe each scene as you go.

7. To store the theatre, fold each end so the theatre is in a flat position.

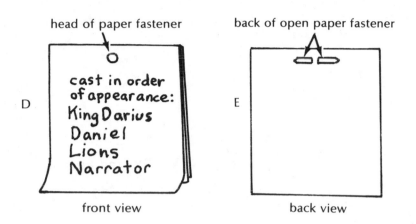

head of paper fastener
back of open paper fastener

D

E

front view
back view

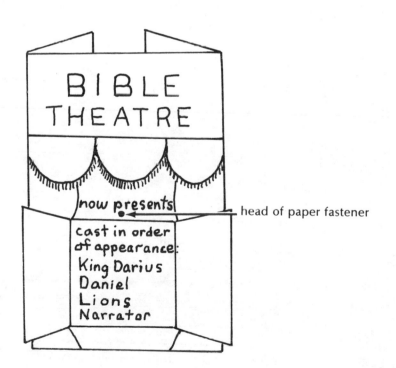

BIBLE THEATRE

now presents

cast in order of appearance:
King Darius
Daniel
Lions
Narrator

head of paper fastener

Jonah and the Whale

Jonah was a prophet who lived in the village of Galilee. God commanded him to go to the city of Ninevah and warn the people that they would be destroyed if they did not stop their evil ways.

Instead of obeying God, Jonah sailed on a ship to Tarshish. God was so angry at Jonah that He created a terrible storm at sea and the sailors feared that they would be shipwrecked. They decided to cast lots to see who was responsible for the storm. The lot fell on Jonah, and he admitted to having disobeyed God. The sailors threw him into the sea, and the water became calm again.

Jonah was swallowed by a whale, and he lived in the darkness in its belly. After three days of praying to God, Jonah was spit up by the whale.

Again God commanded Jonah to warn the people of Ninevah to stop their evil ways. This time he obeyed. The people listened to God's words, prayed for forgiveness, and were saved from destruction.

Since we cannot go back in time and take a picture of Jonah and the whale, let's re-create them through craft projects.

Jonah and the Whale Beanbag Game Wall Hanging

Materials:

1 large solid piece of light-colored material that can be fringed (the size you would like the wall hanging to be)

dowel

small tacks (hardware store)

yarn, any color

pencil

tubes of liquid embroidery, different colors

cardboard

scissors

1 piece of tan or beige unpatterned cotton material

straight pins

thread, color to match nylon tape

needle

small beans or rice

nylon tape fastener, color to match material (fabric store)

Directions:

1. Make a fringe by pulling one thread at a time along all four edges of the material.
2. Attach one edge of the material to the dowel with tacks. Take a long piece of yarn and tie it to each end of the dowel.
3. Using the pencil, draw the story of Jonah and the whale on the material. Number each scene in the order in which it took place. You may wish to use the design in the illustration.
4. Using the liquid embroidery, trace around all the pencilled lines of the design. Optional: Color in all or portions of each picture.
5. To make a Jonah beanbag, draw a simple figure on the cardboard. If you wish, copy the picture of Jonah in the illustration. Keep the proportion of the beanbag to the picture the same as it is in the illustration. Cut out the figure.
6. Fold the tan material in half. Place the cardboard cut-out on the material. Trace around it with the pencil. Cut around the pencil lines, going through both layers of material.
7. Pin the wrong sides of the two pieces of material together.
8. Using tiny stitches, sew the two figures together, leaving a small opening. Remove the pins. Turn the material right side out.
9. Fill the beanbag loosely with the beans. Sew the opening closed.
10. Using the liquid embroidery, draw details such as eyes, hair, mouth, and clothing on the figure.
11. Cut a strip from the nylon tape fastener and sew it across the arms on the back of the beanbag (figure A). Cut another strip of tape the same size, and sew it somewhere on the picture (water, boat, land or whale's mouth).
12. Attach the Jonah beanbag to the wall hanging by pressing the tape on the back of it to the tape on the hanging. To remove Jonah when you play the game, peel the two tapes apart.

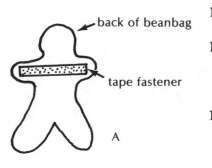

back of beanbag

tape fastener

A

13. How to play the game: Remove the hanging from the wall and place it on the floor. Remove Jonah. Stand several feet from the hanging. Toss the beanbag onto scene number 1. If it lands on the scene, you get another turn and try to toss the beanbag onto scene number 2. The object of the game is to complete all the scenes successfully. If you are "out," the next player has a turn. When your turn comes up again, you must start from number 1. When the game is over, attach Jonah to the material and rehang.

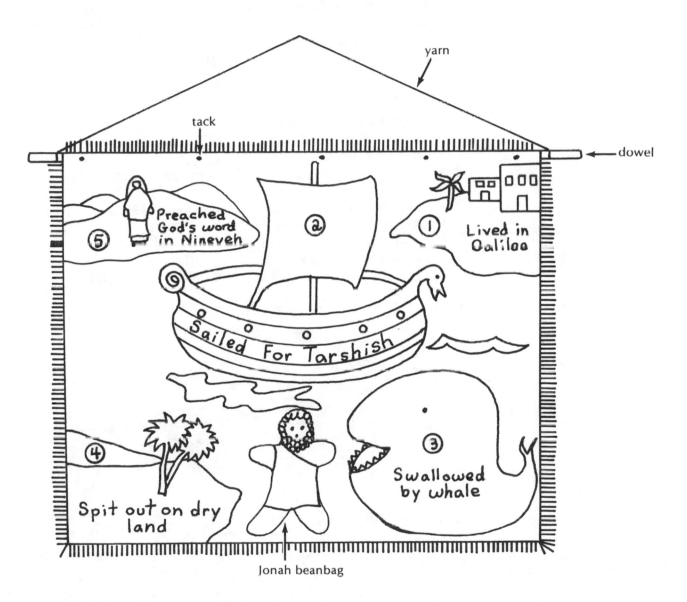

Joanah and the Whale
Whale Mirror

Materials:

piece of wood (pine, hardboard or masonite, plywood, back of paneling)
pencil
coping saw or sabre saw
sandpaper
white base or undercoat (paint store)
paintbrush
enamel paint, any color
special adhesive (glazier store)
permanent felt-tip marking pen, black
mirror (cut to shape by glazier or purchased at a variety store)
glue-on picture hanger

Directions:

1. With the pencil, draw a whale with a wide-open mouth on the surface of the wood. Cut it out with the saw.
2. Sand the edges.
3. Paint one side of the "whale" and the edges with base coat. Don't paint the mouth. Let dry.
4. Paint over the base coat with enamel paint. Let dry.
5. Attach the mirror using the special adhesive.
6. Add eyes with the marking pen.
7. Attach the picture hanger.
8. Look in the mirror and make believe you are Jonah looking out of the whale's mouth.

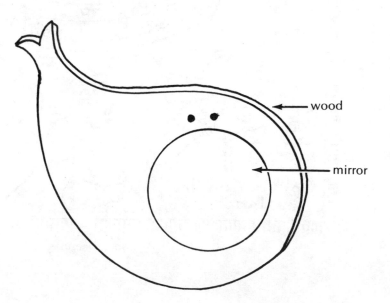

Mobile of Jonah Being Swallowed by the Whale

Materials:

1 small lightweight box with lid (gift box, about 4″ x 6″ (10 cm. x 15 cm.) or small child's shoe box)

scissors or craft knife (craft store)

pencil

glue

felt-tip marking pen, black

heavy cardboard

wide-eyed needle (for heavy thread or yarn)

dowel

Directions:

1. To make the whale's mouth, cut a large hole in one end of the box. Save the cut-out circle for step 2.
2. With the pencil, draw a tail and fins onto the circle. Cut them out and glue them to the box as shown in the illustration.
3. Using the marking pen, draw eyes on the box above the mouth hole, and outline the mouth.
4. With the marking pen, draw the figure of Jonah on the cardboard and cut out. He should be small enough to fit through the mouth of the whale.
5. Thread a piece of string, about 1½′ (0.45 m.) long, through the needle, knotting the long end. Push the needle up through the center of the bottom of the box, coming up through the center of the box lid (figure A). Remove the needle. Tie the protruding string around one end of the dowel.
6. Thread another piece of string, about 2′ (0.6 m.) long, through the needle. Do not make a knot. Keep one end of the string longer

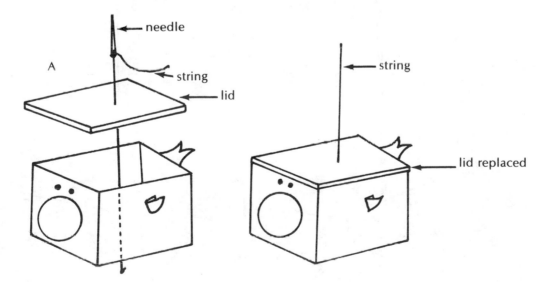

114

than the other. Push the needle through the cardboard Jonah, near the top of his body. Make the ends of the strings even and tie them into a knot. Hang the string on the dowel, moving the string around so that the knot is on top of the dowel. Jonah should hang opposite the whale and level with the whale's mouth.

7. To hang the mobile, tie one end of a string, about 2′ (0.6 m.) long, around the center of the dowel. Tie a loop in the other end and hang the mobile on a doorknob, from a hanging fixture, or tape it to the ceiling. Move the strings on Jonah and the whale back and forth on the dowel, until the mobile balances. To hold the balance, put a drop of glue on each string where it meets the dowel.

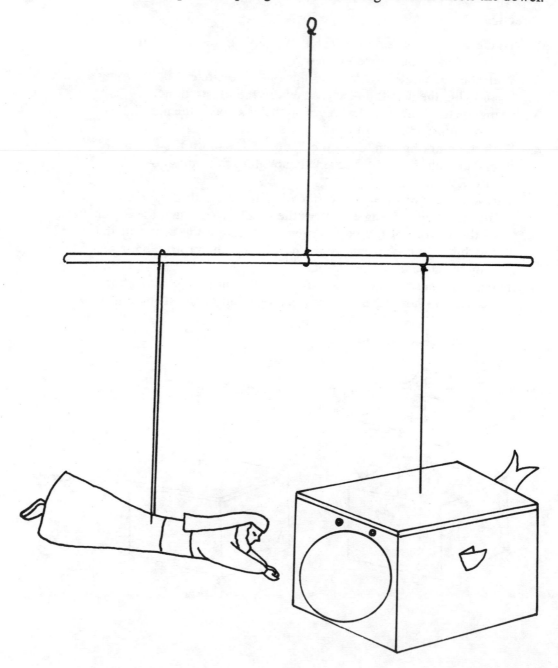

Index

118

About the Author

Joyce Becker is the author/artist of the bestselling books, *Jewish Holiday Crafts* and *Hanukkah Crafts*.

All of the projects in this book have been tested on family and friends, as well as in the creative art classes Mrs. Becker has taught on all age levels during the past twelve years. Her teaching experience includes crafts classes for the mentally retarded at Woodbridge State School in New Jersey. She studied at Pratt Institute and has written and illustrated greeting cards. She is a member of the Writer's Association of New Jersey, and lives in Edison with her husband and their four children.

About the Book

This is an excellent crafts manual for people of all ages who want to make their favorite Bible stories come alive three-dimensionally. There are approximately 75 projects that are organized around 13 Bible stories, from Genesis through the Book of Jonah. Each story is retold in language that young readers especially can appreciate. The crafts are economical, since they involve simple household objects and inexpensive materials that can be purchased at local stores. Many of the projects are decorative, such as a Noah's Ark diorama or a Jonah-and-the-whale mobile. Other items, such as a Garden-of-Eden vase, are useful, and some are just plain fun: a Daniel-in-the-lion's den slide show, a Jacob's ladder movie, and a days-of-creation puzzle.

This book offers a chance to become familiar with some famous Bible stories while expressing oneself creatively. Little or no supervision is necessary, and all the crafts are good fare for a rainy day.

9

63 tire
65-67